Dec. 25, 1955.

With much love for
this X mas season
           to Sister M. A.
                from
     Jeanne Farmer.

LOVE DOES SUCH THINGS

Love
Does Such Things

GOD'S CHRISTMAS GIFT TO MAN

By Rev. M. Raymond, o.c.s.o.

THE BRUCE PUBLISHING COMPANY

MILWAUKEE

NIHIL OBSTAT:

  Fr. M. Thomas Aquinas Porter, O.C.S.O.
  Fr. M. Augustine Westland, O.C.S.O.

IMPRIMI POTEST:

  Fr. M. Gabriel Sortais, O.C.S.O.
  Abbot General

  6 April 1955

NIHIL OBSTAT:

  John A. Schulien, S.T.D.
  Censor librorum

IMPRIMATUR:

  ✝ Albert G. Meyer
  Archiepiscopus Milwauchiensis

  11 August 1955

Rosary College Dewey Classification Number: 232.921

Library of Congress Catalog Card Number: 55-11516

© 1955 by The Bruce Publishing Company
MADE IN THE UNITED STATES OF AMERICA

To

The Mother

of

THE CHRISTMAS CHILD

Mary Immaculate

and

To

A CHILD OF THAT CHRISTMAS MOTHER

Susan Marie Wirth

Foreword

"LOVE DOES SUCH THINGS"

J oy," said Chesterton, "is the secret of the Christian." But not enough Christians know their own secret; and those of us who do know it, have kept it too long and too well. That is why our world is so sad. It does not know — for we have not told it — that all joy lies in the one word "Christmas." But that word must be heard from the lips of God, and understood in the language of God when He says to each human being: "A Merry Christmas to you!"

Oh yes, God says that. And He says it to you. What is more, He means it! If you have not heard Him you cannot possibly know what "merry" means, nor what "Christmas" is. For it is utterly impossible for anyone to have a truly merry Christmas until he has heard God greeting him — and has returned His greeting.

Each year on earth, as December nears its twenty-fifth day, the words "Merry Christmas" are heard everywhere. We hear them on the street, on the streetcar or in the bus, in the stores, at the office, or in the shop. They come to us from our families and friends, from mere acquaintances, and often from sheerest strangers. And the marvelous and some-what mystifying thing about them is that they enjoy, at this season of the year, not only an omnipresence, but some shade and semblance of omnipotence. For though we know they are often spoken merely out of custom and to serve a shallow convention, or only for the sake of commerce, yet they still have within them the secret and unfailing power to lift our hearts. Can you tell how it is that, in the almost limitless compass of our language, there is no other greeting that can begin to compare with the magic that lies in "Merry Christmas!"?

You will never be able to expose the secret of the magic of this greeting until you have heard God saying it and know what He means. Have you ever heard Him? He said it last year and the year before. In fact, He has not failed to say it a single year of your life. For God, you see, never changes, and away back before Time was, He had you in His infinite mind, and was even then not only wishing but actually *willing* you a Merry Christmas!

Of course God has a language all His own, but there is no one who cannot understand it. You must not strain to catch some sound: God speaks by silences. "While all things were in quiet silence, and the night was in the midst of her course, Thy Omnipotent Word, O Lord, came down from Thy royal throne."* Humans greet you with words; but God, with His Only Word, and while humans may favor you with gifts that are personal, God gives you a Gift who is a Person! Humans, at times, speak to you with animation and sincere affection; but God, at all times, speaks to you with a Love that became Incarnate, and in a Passion that was all incarnadined. When God greets you at Christmas, He is not speaking of a day, but of a deed. Any human being can wish you — and even aid you to enjoy — a merry Christmas day. But it is God alone who can *will* it for you, and through a divine Person obtain what He wills: a Christmas that is truly merry because it is recognized to be not a day, not a season, but *Salvation!*

There is the secret of Christian joy. And it is told completely in the word "Christmas."

At Christmas God gives more than a greeting: He gives you a Gift, a Gospel, and a Goal. When an angel spoke to shepherds and gave them the good tidings that "there is born to you a Saviour," he was but interpreting the language

---

* Introit, Mass for Sunday within the Octave of Christmas.

of God for human beings and telling those watchers of the flocks that God was greeting them. But what those men who "went over to Bethlehem and saw those things which had come to pass" could not understand then, you and I can realize fully now; namely, that on the lips of God and in the language of God "Christmas" is a compound word that tells of a Person and a Passion, that speaks of His eternal Word and that Word's ineffable work: that human-divine tragedy which was His and our triumph — the Mass! You and I are in a position to know how true those lines are with which Saul of Tarsus opened his Epistle to the Hebrews: *"God spoke* of old to our ancestors through the prophets; at the present time, . . . *he has spoken to us* through his Son . . ." (Hebr. 1:1).*

Indeed God has spoken. And He has spoken to you and me. But when He says "Christmas," He means *Christ* and His *Mass.* When He says "Merry" He not only wishes us to meet His Christ, but wills that we become His *members;* He not only wishes that we learn about Christ's Mass, but wills that we *live* it. Unless we have heard all that, we have never heard God's greeting. Unless we do all that, we have never returned it; for we have missed the Gospel, rejected the Gift, and will never attain our Goal. For Bishop Jacques Benigné Bossuet never spoke more eloquently than when he said: "There is nothing in the universe greater than Jesus Christ; and nothing in Jesus Christ greater than His loving Sacrifice; and nothing in His loving Sacrifice greater than that last sigh and precious moment which separated His all-adorable soul from His all-adorable Body." And I say that the loving Jesus Christ made that moment eternal and ever present; for when He said "Do this in commemoration of me" He not only ordained His priests and empowered them to say Mass, but gave you a gift that makes every day a Christmas.

---

* Kleist-Lilly translation. Emphasis added.

ix

Christmas is a feast — for most people, the biggest of the year. But Christmas is also a fact — and for all peoples, the greatest of any year. To celebrate the feast aright, we have to grasp the fact. We do that if we hear God greeting us at Christmas. And that we *hear* is eternally important.

If you would hear God just listen quietly to the silences that surround that cave in Bethlehem's chalk hills where a Virgin brings forth a Child in an atmosphere surcharged with the silence of God telling you a long, long story. It is a true story, and one in which you play no minor role. It is a love story, for God knows no other. But like all stories that tell of true love, this is filled with mystery. In it, as in many a good mystery story, there is a murder! But since God deals in romance and not in tragedy, He solves the mystery of this murder by a miracle which scatters all earth's sad clouds, lights up the world's darkness, dries all human tears, as it conquers man's only enemy, the universe's one real evil, and even death itself. "Love leaps the grave" and goes on to prepare for you and me an eternally long, and eternally loving Christmas.

Of course this greeting of God, which brings us face to face with a feast and a fact, brings us also face to face with what baffles our understanding. Why should God ever speak to you or to me? Why should He beggar Himself, as it were, in order to give us at Christmas the gift of His only Son? Why should Bethlehem's Child love us to death — even to the death on the cross? Why?

There is only one answer. It was put into words for Monsignor Romano Guardini, the European philosopher and theologian, as he stood nonplused before evident fact, the same fact that faces us in God's greeting us at Christmas in the form of an Infant. Guardini asked the same question we have asked and knew no answer that would satisfy until a friend said: *Love does such things!* And when that Love is Infinite, what can we not expect?

The Love that does such things has been working a long, long time for you. And when He speaks it is with slowness so that you may hear aright. When He greets you at Christmas it is with a single Word whose every letter is of eternal import.

Let us spell it out together.

Contents

LOVE DOES SUCH THINGS

ST. ANNE AND THE VIRGIN
BY BARTOLOME ESTABAN MURILLO
PRADO, MADRID, SPAIN

Shepherds and Sheep Help You
Hear God Speaking

S is the first letter of the one word God uses to greet you at Christmas. It blazes as did that bush Moses once saw all aflame yet not being one bit consumed. Approach this letter now as he approached that bush then; for you are to hear exactly what Moses heard: *the voice of God.* It will be speaking not only directly to you, but it will be talking about you. It will tell you truths as personal as your pulse, as intimate as your breathing, and far more important than your bodily breath.

The letter has to do with *self* — both God Him*self,* and you your*self.* But to learn how literally true that is, you will first let it stand for shepherds and sheep. Then, as you carefully spell on, you will come to see that God, who has been thinking of you and your Christmas from all eternity, has had a shepherd and a sheep ever in His mind; and hereafter, whenever you think of sheep or shepherds you will think of God — and hear His Christmas greeting to you.

Unless you differ greatly from most mortals, you have lived your life from day to day almost utterly unmindful of the wondrous fact that you are immortal. If you should be asked this moment: "How long have you lived?" would your instantaneous reply be: "As long as God!"? It should be; for that is the literal truth. And you should be ready

3

and happy to add: "And I shall go on living as long as God goes on loving." That is the reality that lifts your heart, fills your world with sunshine, and frees you from every fear. Never should it come home to you with greater force or fuller clarity than when you hear the word "Christmas"; for that is the word which tells you exactly what you are worth in the eyes of God. It is a word which holds in its heart the loveliest romance that has ever been recorded. It is your life-story. And it is God who has done the telling — in a single word!

You need to know your own worth if you are to live a happy life. But never will you come to that knowledge until you arrive at the realization that almighty God has been thinking of you ever since He has been — and He is without beginning! He is a jealous God. He told you so Himself when He gave Moses the Ten Commandments, which are really laws of love. But there is only one thing of which He is truly jealous — and that is His own glory. Everything else He will give away. Everything else He has given away. But His glory is the one thing of which He says: ". . . *alteri non dabo.*" That, He will not give to another. And you are inextricably involved in His glory. So He is jealously in love with you. That is why there is a Christmas. But to grasp all this you must spell out the word God uses with all the care at your command. Begin as God begins, not as so many moderns do. He begins with "S" — it had to do with sheep and a shepherd, but not with the ones you most frequently see and hear about today.

Look at your Christmas cards, listen to your Christmas carols, go to a Christmas play, or view the Christmas story as presented on TV today, and you will see that it is practically impossible to think of Christmas without, at the same time, thinking of shepherds and sheep. But they are always the shepherds who watched near Bethlehem, and the sheep are the sheep of their flocks. It is a legitimate way to begin the

L
G-O-D
V
E

4

Christmas story, but it is not the way God began. Hence, if you begin your spelling with these shepherds and sheep you will never learn how long you have lived nor how long you have been loved; for you will not be told how persistent God has been in His Christmas greetings to you.

Who were the first humans to hear God speaking of Christmas? Who was the first angel to whom God spoke about Christmas for you? The impulse is to name Gabriel as the angel and Mary, Joseph, and the shepherds of Bethlehem as the ones of earth. Both replies are wrong. God did not begin to think of you and your Christmas joy when He first sent Gabriel to Mary — or even when He sent him to Zachary to announce the birth of John the Baptist, that "angel who was to go before the face of Christ." God was thinking of you and your Christmas centuries before Bethlehem shepherds were born. And all down those centuries, and on to this present day, God worked that you might have a Merry Christmas. So it is well to learn just who were the first to hear God saying anything about you and your Christmas joys.

Of course there is justification for modern authors, commercial artists, playwrights, and composers of carols to give you as opening scene for the Christmas mystery an arch of night sky chilled with stars, a dark plain broken by the red glow of a tiny fire, around which gather men whose work it is to watch the flocks. Their sheep are usually shown huddled a grayish-white blur in the background. It is God's Gospel according to St. Luke that furnishes us with the details of this silent scene of deep calm and utter peace. The physician-evangelist has created an atmosphere of holy hush with his stars, shepherds, and sheep. Soon he splits the darkness with the radiant glory of God and breaks that deep silence with those angelic words: "Fear not!" as prelude to the "good tidings of great joy." Yet, though that is God's Gospel and that the beginning of the Christmas story to be found therein, it is not the way God began to speak to you of Christmas!

THE FIRST TIME

L
G-O-D
V
E

5

Nor was Gabriel, great Angel though he be of the Annunciation and the Incarnation, the first angelic spirit to hear God speaking of Christ and Christmas.

To learn that angel's name you have to go back far beyond the time of Zachary and look upon a scene far different from that on the hillside near Bethlehem. If you are to tell the Christmas story in anything like chronological order, you cannot begin with "Once upon a time . . ." You must begin with "Once upon eternity . . ." For what the Church takes from the Book of Proverbs and applies to Mary of Nazareth, can in all truth be taken and applied to you. Of yourself you can say: "The Lord possessed me in the beginning of his ways, before he made anything from the beginning. I was set up from eternity, and of old before the earth was made. The depths were not as yet, and I was already conceived, neither had the fountains of water as yet sprung out. The mountains with their huge bulk had not as yet been established: before the hills I was brought forth" (Prov. 8:22–25). That is literally true of you; for your Christmas story really begins with: "Once upon eternity, God fell in love with you. . . ."

That is why you will not take Matthew's stately prose giving you that genealogy of Jesus, which simply mesmerizes the student of Sacred History, as you begin to spell out God's word. Nor will St. Mark entice you with that mysterious prophecy about the "angel that shall go before the face of God and be a Voice crying in the Wilderness"; a prophecy which he attributes to Isaias, but which you will find more fully in Malachias. St. Luke's two lovely chapters have enchanted mankind since the day they were first penned under the watchful eye of God the Holy Ghost and the promptings of the motherly memory of Mary Immaculate. But if you are limited to the Gospels for your chronological beginning you will go to the theologian among the Evangelists, and you will begin as does St. John: *In principio erat Verbum* . . . "In the beginning was the Word, and the Word was with God; and the

L
G-O-D
V
E

6

Word was God . . . All things were made through Him . . . In Him was life, and the life was the light of men. And the light shines in the darkness . . ." On you will go in that same prologue to the last Gospel until you reach that climax which sends all men of faith to their knees in holy awe and loving adoration: ". . . And the Word was made Flesh, and dwelt among us" (Prologue, Jn. 1–14).

Yes, you must go back to the beginning, "to the unbeginning of endlessness and Eternity." For God has loved you with an everlasting love, and has had Christmas thoughts about you from that timeless moment He decreed to create. Yet there was a moment of time when an angel and two human beings heard the voice of God speaking for the first time about Christmas — and God was thinking of you. It happened in a Garden when life was very young, just after sin had been committed for the first time by any human being.

But here you must be warned. Since God is Love, and has been in love with you from all eternity, you need not think that He would never have greeted you on the Birthday of the Christ had not Adam listened to Eve after she had listened to the Serpent. No. With a whole school of subtle theologians, with saints such as Bernard of Siena and Francis de Sales, with the great and holy Suarez, you can well believe that there would have been a Christ even if there had never been any "forbidden fruit." But there would have been this tremendous difference: you would not now be hearing of sheep and shepherds, nor would you know how strong is the love of your God nor how infinitely resourceful is your Infinite Lover. For while you would have had *Christ,* His name would not have been *Jesus.* And while God could have wished you the "Happy Commemoration of the Birthday of the Babe," He could never have greeted you in the way He does now. You would have had God who became Man, but you would never know that He loved you to death; for there would have been no *Mass.* You would have Christ but no Christ*mas.*

L
G-O-D
V
E

7

Oh, how all heaven must have gasped in awe as those Nine Angelic Choirs heard God speak out in the Garden of Eden, in the presence of the two shamefaced humans, and address that angel named Lucifer with a condemnation and a curse that was the first mention of Christ and Christmas. God was thinking of you as He said to Satan: "I will put enmities between thee and the woman, and thy seed and her seed; she shall crush thy head, and thou shalt lie in wait for her heel" (Gen. 3:15). He was also thinking of a shepherd, a sheep, and all that is connoted by them. In all truth God was saying to Adam and Eve what Gabriel was one night to say to Bethlehem shepherds: "Fear not! For I bring you good tidings of great joy." Yes, God was saying in effect "Merry Christmas" to your first mother and father, and through them to you. They did not know it then. You may not fully realize it now. So go on spelling carefully. But remember this first letter "S" does not stand for Sin, Shame, Satan, or Serpent. Nor does God's greeting now mark the beginning of your divine Romance. It is but a turning point and proves that God was determined with all the determination of His omnipotent will to love you to death; to beggar Himself if need be to win your little heart. With a resourcefulness possible only in an infinite Lover He had devised a way that would call for miracle after miracle, pile mystery upon mystery, but was calculated to pluck at your heartstrings with an irresistible tenderness.

But how Gabriel, Michael, Raphael, and all the rest of the loyal angels of God must have marveled! They had seen Lucifer sin once and be hurled like a thunderbolt from heaven's threshold into hell. Could they expect anything less for these First Parents of yours who were so far less a creation than Lucifer and his followers since they were made of spirit and clay?

GOD'S
CAREFUL
ACCENT

The one explanation of this almost infinite difference we have already seen: *Love does such things.* God, who is Love, will use infinite resourcefulness to save you for Himself.

8

Too seldom do you accent the second syllable of Christmas. But God, in greeting you, stresses that syllable. And when you listen closely you will observe that, unlike us, He lengthens the "i" in the first syllable of the word, thus giving the full and sacred significance to the word of all words for us.

Look at your Christmas cards and count if you can the number of times you come across representations of a lone lamb — or of whole flocks of sacrificial sheep. What commercial artists have placed on their greeting cards — and which too many moderns look at and characterize as "silly" — you can only regard as sacred; for you know that God, in His many books of the Bible, which can be read as His greeting card to you, has mentioned shepherds, sheep, and lambs almost incessantly. One of the earliest lines in Genesis tells of the first human who was to taste death, and it says of him that he "was a shepherd." One of the last lines of the Apocalypse speaks of a Lamb that "was slain from the beginning of the world" and who is the Lamp of that City of God which is your heavenly home. Those two lines, distant as they are from each other in time and in God's great Book, are nevertheless intimately related and have to do with you and your happiness at Christmas. For the first man to die was symbol of Him "who lives forever" and who is your very life. God seems to do just the opposite to what we humans would do. He makes a man a symbol of an animal, and an animal the One symbolized by the man. But in that reversal of what we would ordinarily expect, God is tenderly telling you how much He loves you and is making His whole universe eloquent of His Christmas greeting. Since God speaks in types and symbols and figures, the cheapest little Christmas card with its representation of a lamb or sheep is rich in mystic meaning; for it will tell you what not only the Gospels of Jesus Christ tell you, but what the other larger, longer books of God's great Bible tell you.

St. Paul, in opening his Epistle to the Hebrews says that "In many fragmentary and varying utterances God spoke of

L
G-O-D
V
E

9

old. . . ." It is true. Yet there is unity in that variety, and a wholeness to those fragments. The letter "S" and all it signifies will enable you to grasp what God has done from Abel to the end of the Apocalypse: He has focused on Christ who is the Lamb of God and your own Good Shepherd!

The death of the first man on earth pulses with personal meaning for you and your attainment of eternal life. This murder of Abel by his own brother is actually part of your Christmas story. Read that chapter of Genesis and hear God's Christmas greetings to you; for Abel was a figure of Him whose birthday you celebrate December twenty-fifth. The fact that he was a shepherd who sacrificed lambs to God, and whose sacrifice was highly acceptable to Omnipotence, ought to tell you much about God's Christmas greeting and God's Christmas gift! The further fact that Abel was done to death by his own brother ought to serve as amplifier for the Voice of God and enable you to catch with ease the careful and clear articulation of God's personal greeting to you, and to evaluate properly the stress He places on the second syllable of the word Christmas.

How pointedly it comes out in the Gospel! St. Matthew opens his account of the Christmas story with the genealogy of Jesus. As you read it from Abraham to Joseph you hear the recurring bleating of sheep and the pipes of shepherds. Abraham, Isaac, and Jacob, those Patriarchs of God's Chosen People, and your own spiritual ancestors, were watchers of flocks. Of course one reason for this was economical: sheep were needed to sustain physical life. But do not think for a moment that that is the whole reason. Sheep were needed even more to express spiritual life! Men may want for words with which to tell God they adore Him, to speak out their love and appreciation of His gifts, or even to ask for what they yet need. But so long as men have lambs they can burn as holocausts they will ever be eloquent in adoring, thanking, praising, and petitioning God. That is why God's greeting and gift to you is

L
G-O-D
V
E

10

the lovable Lamb of God who is named at the end of this long line of keepers of the sheep. That is also why the word "Christmas" must ever break up into its components for you, and every representation of a sheep or a shepherd enable you to hear God speaking to you of His *Christ* and Christ's *Mass*.

The Lamb of God — His Christmas gift to you — was to be laid in a manger which stood in a cave that had been hollowed out of one of the chalk hills near Bethlehem. That cave and manger are really the center of your world. Almighty God was the sculptor. Year after slow year, with wind and rain, He sculptured. Only in the fullness of time did He consider His work finished. It took Him centuries to arch the roof to that span which would allow the bleat of the Lamb to sound down all future centuries so that no one born of woman might ever say he was without a perfect Christmas gift. He worked aeons to make the entrance wide enough for all mankind. And during all this time He had you in mind! It is not often you think of wind and rain as instruments in the hands of God who is working for you. But now that you have been reminded how the Cave was fashioned, every storm of wind and every shower of rain will be the Voice of God speaking lovingly to you. And when you find yourself in the midst of spiritual storms, you will know that God is hollowing out a befitting birthplace for His Son, sculpturing a cave where His Christ may be born anew — within you. Never forget that your soul is a capacity for God and nothing else. Since He labored so long and lovingly over the cave in which Jesus was to stay for but a few hours, how, think you, will He labor over that soul of yours which is to hold Jesus all the days of your life? Every day is Christmas Day — for Christ is born anew.

St. Luke tells us that Mary "wrapped him in swaddling clothes, and laid him in a manger" (Lk. 2–7). You have just learned that a cloud in the sky and a wind across a field are instruments of God. You can safely conclude that everything

WHO BUILT
THE CAVE

L
G-O-D
V
E

11

that happens is part of His all-wise plan. God made the manger for His Lamb. But He did so through the calloused hands of some Bethlehem shepherd who was only intent on fulfilling the ordinary task of his calling.

A simple shepherd, a practical man of the pastures, who had herded his sheep into a certain cave in Bethlehem's hillsides whenever it stormed, one day eyed a shelf of that chalky rock which makes those hillsides and decided to hollow it out to serve as trough to hold fodder for his lambs and sheep. Soon he was at work; how the Triune God and the Nine Angelic Choirs must have watched him as he worked! Long before he was finished with the task you can be sure he found it humdrum and monotonous. But he chipped away at that chalky substance until he had what he wanted — a hollow that would hold feed for his flock. But unknown to himself he had labored not only with God but for God. And his every hammer stroke will sound down the arches of the years unto the trump of Doom; for each blow contributed to the shaping of that bed upon which the ineffable and eternal God was laid as a newborn Babe.

Life can never be the same once you have looked on that lone shepherd and seen him achieve a double effect with a single work. He not only readied a manger for his bleating sheep; he shaped a crib for the very Lamb of God. And you, as you now toil at your daily tasks, must wonder what extraordinary thing you are accomplishing for God, as you achieve something ordinary for yourself. These truths about the cave and the crib bring God so very near! The Burning Bush is throwing its heat in your face. Your hills are being covered with holy cloud. You see God's hand not only on the stars in their courses, you hear the beat of His heart not only in the ever sounding sea, but you feel His very breath upon your cheek. Divine Providence has been made all but tangible. You have learned that it is more than general, governing the whole world; more even than particular, having special regard for

L
G-O-D
V
E

12

men; you have learned it is personal — that in all truth God is ever acting for you. The realization sets your whole soul singing. But to make your song a proper Christmas carol, let it be a shepherd's song.

The meticulous St. Matthew in giving the genealogy of Jesus names David before Abraham. His opening line runs: "A record of the life of Jesus Christ, the Son of David, the Son of Abraham." That is no accident; for there are no accidents with God, and the Gospels are God's books. David was a shepherd of Bethlehem, a singing shepherd, from whom you will learn your Christmas song. Could anything be more fitting? Was not Jesus born in David's town, of David's line, and destined, as Gabriel foretold, to inherit David's throne? Did not Jesus speak of Himself as David's Son, and tell carping high priests and elders that day of triumphal entry that if He stopped the children from hosanna-ing Him as David's Son the very rocks would tell the world that He was of David's line? Because David was a shepherd of Bethlehem it is not impossible that he often herded his sheep into the very cave where Christ was born. You may even picture this singer of Psalms seated at the mouth of that cave as he composes what we have labeled Psalm 22 — which will serve you all the days of your life as the perfect Christmas carol.

It is a lilting *pastorale* that breathes with the beauty of all outdoors. It is a song that sings of peace and plenty and protection. It is a prayer of thanksgiving and of praise that you can take to your heart and hum forever in your soul; for it is a song about you and your God. It will give you that imperturbable peace which the angel proclaimed that first Christmas night. Let the stars fall, the suns all burn out, the earth itself wither away, you can still sing with David:

> The Lord is my shepherd, and nothing do I want: he bids me
>   to repose in verdant pastures;
> to springs where I may rest he leads me on, and there refreshes
>   me.

YOUR CHRISTMAS CAROL

L
G-O-D
V
E

He leads me onward over safe, straight paths to manifest His
holy name.

And should I cross a gloomy vale, no evil shall I fear, because
you are with me.

Your crook and staff — they comfort me (Ps. 22).*

That was first sung by a man who had never heard Christ
tell the parable of the Good Shepherd, nor say to Peter as
He gave him the Primacy: "Feed my lambs. Feed my sheep."
It was composed by a shepherd who had never heard the
Christ pray "that there might be but one Fold and One Shepherd"; who had never heard the bleating of the newborn Lamb
of God. Yet, see how perfectly he has spelled the Word you
are now slowly spelling out! See how fully he has grasped all
that is suggested by the letter "S." And since God has greeted
you with a Gift how you must sing: "The Lord is my Shepherd,
and nothing do I want." You don't. You can't. For since the
bleat of God's Lamb went out over Bethlehem's chalk hills,
you, though you might be wanting everything — home, work,
food, clothes, friends — lack absolutely nothing that is necessary
for your eternal merry Christmas! That is the secret of happiness in Time and for Eternity. God has given you a Gift which
you can literally call perfect — and of which you can truthfully
say: "It was just what I wanted" — meaning "of what I had
need!"

You were born in exile. Your earthly parents were DP's.
But neither they nor you could ever get back to your native
land; for more than continents and seas, more than the measureless stretches of interstellar space yawned between you and
your proper home. The distance was infinite. Sin made it that
way. You were far more destitute than that Prodigal of whom
we read that he "would fain fill his belly with the husks the
swine did eat" (Lk. 15:16). You had no way of rising and
going back to your Father's house. You were a stray sheep,
completely lost, totally lacking the ability to get back to the

L
G-O-D
V
E

---

* Kleist-Lynam translation.

fold. . . . Indeed you can sing as a Christmas carol: "The Lord is my Shepherd . . ." He sought you out. He found you! You have just learned something of how He called into play His Omnipotence, not only to shape a manger, but to bring forth the miracle of the Man who is God, and the God who is a Lamb for Sacrifice! It caused Him to compound a word with which He might greet and gift you: *Christ* and *Mass*.

"S," the first letter of God's word, tells you of your Good Shepherd and His utterly unblemished Lamb; it tells you that He was the Sheep for your Sacrifice, and that His Sacrifice was your salvation! God has reason for the adjective before His substantive. He not only wishes; He *wills* you a joyful Christmas!

Go on with your spelling. The second letter in His word is the first in our alphabet.

L
G-O-D
V
E

15

THE ANNUNCIATION

BY FRA FILIPPO LIPPI

NATIONAL ART GALLERY, WASHINGTON, D. C.

Angels Announce God's
Tidings to You

A is the second letter you meet as you carefully spell out God's word. It stands for angels!

If the first letter was likened to the Burning Bush whence Moses heard the very voice of God, this one can be compared only to "the pillar of cloud that stood at the door of the tabernacle when the Lord spoke to Moses face to face, as a man is wont to speak to his friend" (Exod. 33:10, 11). For while sheep and shepherds have revealed much of your "tremendous Lover" — God — to you, angels with their annunciations will reveal even more, as they tell you truths about yourself, concerning which you, perhaps, have never even dreamed.

The first letter set you singing a shepherd's song about Divine Providence, as it increased your faith. This second letter will not only keep you singing that Psalm of David as your continuous Christmas carol, but will quicken the tempo and clarify the tone as it sets hope surging in your soul like some crystal fountain whose limpid waters rise, arch over gracefully, and shower your world with God's silver-white gladness.

Time — unmeasured lengths of it — has moved on since God first spoke in the Garden and told of that combat and conquest which really spell Christmas; for we know that God, as He spoke, had a Sheep and Shepherd in mind. The moon has

17

tugged at the tides of the seven seas perhaps billions on billions of times, and the four seasons have rounded their full wheel through thousands and thousands of centuries since God first began His sculpturing of the cave where Christ was born. And never once did that moon wax or wane, or any summer wither into autumn without God having you in mind. But now that the seventy weeks of Daniel have run their course and the "fullness of time" has come, God will speak to you. But this time it will not be to an angel, but through one. Oh, the delicate courtesy of God! It was through the whispering of an angel to a woman that every grave the world has seen was dug, every human tear salted, and the very terror of the H-bomb prepared. Michael, Gabriel, Raphael, and the rest of the angelic host blushed over that fact. That one of their own who had rebelled against God should have led humans into a like rebellion caused them intense shame. But now God would prove Himself not only forgiving but even chivalrous toward the angelic world as, instead of speaking Himself in this highest of high moments in the history of God and man, He selects an angel — one of the greatest — to go down to Galilee, to a town called Nazareth, to whisper to a woman who was, like Eve, a virgin, and like Eve, destined to become the Mother of all the living, but unlike Eve, to do so without tarnishing her virginity.

This was in the "fullness of time" and rightly is it named the highest of all high moments in history. Now you are to know it as the loveliest hour of your life. For in all truth *you were there!* God sent Gabriel to you to greet you in Mary. This greeting has been named "The Annunciation," and stands rightly as the First of the Joyful Mysteries that mark your Rosary. But it is just as right to name it "God's love call to you!" — and "God's call to you to love!" For that is precisely what "Merry Christmas" means when it is fully understood as it falls from the lips of God.

Twentieth-century Americans give little thought to angels,

L
G-O-D
V
E

18

and less to Annunciations. Yet in the long history of mankind
— and even of God — no moment is of greater import than the
one which saw an Angel announce to the Maid of Nazareth
named Mary, that she was to be the Mother of God.

That fact, coupled with its consequence — God's becoming
man — staggers the intellect and sets the whole mental world
whirling until you recall again that "Love does such things!"
Yes, love sends angels to make announcements. Think often of
these ministers and messengers of God, these soaring flames of
adoration, these fires of love and burning praise. Can you step
out into a star-studded Christmas Eve and head toward Midnight Mass without hearing the very whir of their wings? Or
if it is in the dark just before the dawn that you make your
way to the miracle and marvel we call the Mass, you can be
sure your east is silvered by "a multitude of the heavenly host
singing 'Glory to God in the heavens above, and on earth
peace to men of good will'" (Lk. 2:13).*

A brother of Gabriel — that angel of Christmas, of the
Annunciation and the Incarnation — is bending over your
shoulder as you read this book. Another is watching over your
family; a third has the duty of protecting your Church, your
parish, and your diocese; a fourth has been appointed to care
for your city; a fifth, for your state; and you can be sure
there is a powerful angel guarding your nation. For your
nation, state, city, diocese, parish, Church, family, and *self* are
dear to God, important parts of His plan, as necessary as was
the lone shepherd who shaped the crib, and the winds and
rains that fashioned the cave; as necessary — let it be said with
awe — as that lovely Lady who gave her flesh and blood to
form the Christ.

Small wonder angels surround you! For God made you in
His own image and likeness — and angels minister unto God
and all things that belong to Him. Smaller wonder that

ANGELS ARE
ALL ABOUT
YOU

L
G-O-D
V
E

---

* Kleist-Lilly translation.

Gabriel's brothers attend you. For you were created to do, in your own way, what Mary Immaculate did in hers: make it possible for God to Sacrifice unto God *in Christ Jesus,* that the weary of the world might have wine, the famished of mankind have bread, and our sinful earth know, not only Christ, but Christmas.

Do you find your credulity strained by such a statement as: God sent Gabriel to you? Do you marvel that you should be told that you, in your way, are to do what only Mary did: Mother Christ? Then study Gabriel's last words to Mary: "Nothing indeed is impossible with God" (Lk. 1:36).* Recall again that "Love does such things." Remember you are spelling out the word God uses to greet you at Christmas. And never forget that on the lips of God that greeting is all love. Now love is always a call to things much above our petty selves. It holds a hidden command to unquestioning sacrifice. It is a challenge to our generosity, calling, as it does, for a total unselfing of self and a complete consecration to another. It is an invitation to heroism. And somehow or other, it is one we never hesitate to answer. When that call comes from God through the annunciation of an angel, our lips form the single word *Fiat.* It is the only way we can return God's Christmas greeting in a single word. Mary did it — and you were there! You did it in her!

This second letter takes you from Bethlehem — the House of Bread — where you have seen a cave readied for "the living Bread that comes down from Heaven" and a manger prepared for that Manna which will sustain us all in this wilderness of the world and be Viaticum as we make our way through this wilderness back to our heavenly home. It brings you to Nazareth, which can be interpreted as "flowering place." It is the place where flowered the Lily of Israel, the fairest flower earth has ever seen. It is the place destined from all eternity to see

L
G-O-D
V
E

* Kleist-Lilly translation.

the root of Jesse bring forth what will one day be the Passion Flower, the only bloom that can grace your altar and give you a merry Christ-Mass! Its seeding was done when Gabriel winged his way from the throne of God with the message of all messages for you and your joy in time and for eternity.

Gabriel has been represented as concentrating on the words he would use in order to win Mary's consent. The author's fancy is understandable when we study the actual message and realize that the fate of the entire universe hung on the lips of this peasant girl of Nazareth, who at most was fourteen years of age at the time. Luke's narration, which came from the lips of Mary, shows clearly that Gabriel made a perfect speech: he won attention from the very start, then swept on to his proposition and proof, to end with what would be utterly persuasive. How his opening words must have riveted Mary's attention on him! "Hail, thou who art full of grace"; then, as if that would not hold the attention of any woman, he adds: "the Lord is with thee," which certainly is enough to render the most indifferent utterly benevolent. But Gabriel is not done yet with his introduction. He adds: "blessed art thou among women."

With Mary's astonished and somewhat perplexed eyes upon him, Gabriel reassures her: "Do not be afraid; thou hast found favor in the sight of God." Then, as the Maiden showed more ease, the angel went on with his annunciation: "Behold thou shalt conceive in thy womb, and shalt bear a son, and shalt call him Jesus." It was done! God had given His Christmas greetings in clearest terms; for that name, which is above all names, bespeaks the Mass. And God said "Christ" as Gabriel went on with his annunciation: "He shall be great, and shall be called the Son of the Most High; and the Lord God will give him the throne of David his father, and he shall be king over the house of Jacob forever; and of his kingdom there shall be no end." What a message for *you*. Sing your Shepherd

L
G-O-D
V
E

Song. It is your Christmas carol. "The Lord is my Shepherd; and nothing do I want" (Lk. 1:32–33). How can you when God is giving you "the Son of the most High"?

Mary questioned the angel, you know; not in doubt, but in firmest belief. Her interrogation of Gabriel really holds her reply to him. She was asking only the way in which all this was to be accomplished. She got her answer in a rush as God's messenger told her: "The Holy Spirit shall come upon thee, and the power of the Most High shall overshadow thee; and therefore the Holy One to be born shall be called the Son of God" (Lk. 1:35–36). Could anyone doubt the words of John the Evangelist that "God is Love" after reading that message of Gabriel? But the breathless scene is far from ended. Gabriel would close his annunciation with a revelation that would thrill the womanly heart of Mary and convince her beyond every possibility of doubt that Christmas was at hand. "And behold, Elizabeth thy kinswoman also has conceived a son in her old age, and she who was called barren is now in her sixth month; for nothing shall be impossible with God" (Lk. 1:28–38).

The first human had heard the clear enunciation of God's Christmas greetings. But as yet no human had returned His greetings. Gabriel now stood waiting to see if he could go back to heaven with a reply that would not only make the heart of God glad, but give cause for every human heart to beat with higher hope and much higher love. God's love call had been sounded. Would you and humanity give reply? Oh you were there — in Mary! As St. Thomas of Aquin has so lucidly taught "it was announced to Mary that she was to conceive the Christ so that the spiritual wedlock between the Son of God and human nature might be manifest. The Virgin's consent was sought in lieu of the whole human race." That is why it can be said so unqualifiedly that you were there; that God sent Gabriel to you; that Mary gave assent for you.

L
G-O-D
V
E

22

St. Bernard of Clairvaux tells what that assent means when he says: "Behold the Angel now awaits thy answer . . . We, also, O Lady, await from thy lips the sentence of mercy and compassion, we who are so miserably groaning under the sentence of condemnation. For lo! the price of our salvation is now offered to thee: if thou wilt only consent, we shall at once be set at liberty. We have been created by the Eternal Word of the Father, and behold we die; by thy momentary word we must be renewed and restored to life. O Virgin most loving, Adam, now exiled from Paradise with all his suffering offspring, implores this favor of thee. For it, Abraham entreats thee, and David, and all the other holy fathers, thine own ancestors, who are now dwelling in the region of the shadow of death. See the whole world, prostrate at thy feet, awaits thy answer. And with reason! For on thy word depends the consolation of the miserable, the redemption of the captive, the pardon of the condemned, the salvation of every child of Adam, of the entire human race. O Virgin, delay not to reply. Speak the word, O Lady; speak the word which all on earth, and all in limbo, yes, and even all in Paradise are waiting to hear. Christ Himself, the King and Lord of all, longs for thy answer with a longing equal to the ardor wherewith He 'hath desired thy beauty,' because it is by means of thy consent that He has decreed to save the world."

Do you see how rightly the Annunciation has been called "a hushed moment in the history of the universe when the fate of the world hung on the response of a little girl"? Do you also see Mary's unquestionably essential contribution to your Christmas?

St. Bernard went on in that same sermon to describe God's love call in these words: "For behold Christ calls to thee from Heaven, saying, 'O fairest among women, let thy voice sound in my ears.'" And the Saint pleads with Mary: "If thou wilt give Him to hear thy voice, He will give thee to see our salvation. . . . Art thou she to whom this has been promised or 'look

ON THE
WORD OF
A WOMAN

L
G-O-D
V
E

we for another'? Nay, thou thyself art she, and there is none other. Thou art she who has been promised, been expected, been yearned for . . . Thou art she in whom and by whom 'God our King before the ages hath decreed to work salvation in the midst of the earth.' . . . Make haste, therefore, to answer the Angel, or rather, to answer the Lord through the Angel. Say the word and receive the Word. Utter thy human word and conceive the Divine Word. Pronounce a transitory word and embrace the Word Everlasting. . . . Why dost thou hesitate? . . . Behold the Desired of all the nations is standing outside and knocking at thy door. Oh, if He should pass on whilst thou delayest to open! . . . Arise, make haste to open to Him. Arise by faith, make haste by devotion, open by consent."*

And Mary said *Fiat*. . . .

There is the word which brought the universe into being when it fell from the lips of God. It brought God Himself into flesh when it fell from the lips of Mary. It will bring Christ into your soul with the Father and the Holy Ghost, it will bring sanctity's sunshine into all your world, and the everlasting God into all your passing relations when it falls from your lips. It will make your life an endless Christmas.

Angels with their annunciations tell you the tenderness of your God's heart. He could have commanded Mary. He could command you. But no. An angel must be sent whose salutation forms the loveliest prayer we know. And both Christ and His Mass — Christmas — depend on the free will of a girl still in her early teens! Omnipotence awaits the word of a frail young woman. Omniscience is eager to learn what a finite mind will answer. And all that you might have a Babe to love and call "Jesus" — which means Saviour!

SHE SAID "YES" TO GOD

And what was Mary asked to give that the whole universe — earth, limbo, heaven itself — needed? Her consent! An act of her will allowing God to have His way in her flesh and blood.

---

* Fourth Sermon on *"Missus Est"* — author's translation.

How simple a thing! Yet on it depended the joy of every generation, the happiness — be it said with awe and reverence — of God Himself. Mary said "Yes," to God — and God found that tiny spot in His world whence He could come forth and make Christmas. God asked that tiny bit of Mary. He asks the same of you today for the very same purpose. He never changes. He is as delicate, tender, and chivalrous today with you as He was with the angels and Mary at the Annunciation. Daily, hourly, almost every moment Gabriel is at your side — with an annunciation.

From gospel accounts it would seem that Gabriel has only one message. It always begins with "Fear not!" That is what he said to Zachary when he made the annunciation of the miraculous conception and birth of John the Baptist; that is what he said to Mary when he announced the more miraculous conception and foretold the birth of Jesus; that is what he said — if he, as so many think, was the angel — when God announced to Joseph that he was to take Mary as his wife, for the Child that she carried had been conceived by the Holy Ghost; that is what he said when he announced the birth of your Good Shepherd and your Lamb for Sacrifice — your Christ-Mass — to Bethlehem shepherds. His "Fear not!" was always followed by "good tidings" which always brought "great joy." All that is inevitable; for Gabriel is only a minister and a messenger of God, and could your God give you anything but good tidings that would bring great joy? Could He send you anything that would arouse fear? Gabriel is at your side every moment of your day. He has good tidings; they bring great joy, if you imitate Mary and say "Yes," to God. For that will give Him the room in the world that He wants. See how important Mary was to God? And how important you are?

Angels with their annunciations explain you to yourself. They tell you truths the weary world, with its absorption in matter and time, never dreams of.

At Christmastide every normal person feels bigger, better,

L
G-O-D
V
E

more himself or herself. You dimly realize that you are more in love with God and much more in love with your fellow humans — at least for a few days. Actually you have an expansion of heart and mind and emotions. You *are* a bigger and better person at this season, because Gabriel and his brother angels with their annunciations assure you that at Christmastide you are more nearly your true self. God not only made you great; He made you to be great and to do great things for Him and your fellow man. God, being God, could not do otherwise. But men make themselves, and try to make all other men, small. God wants you to share in His infinity; to live as He lives and love as He loves. That is the ultimate meaning of His Christmas greeting to you. Let Gabriel alert you to the fact that your destiny, your being's heart and home is with infinity — and only there!

Never think yourself anything but *tremendous*. Almighty God depends on you. Without your consent His Christ cannot be born anew. The weary of the world will not have their Wine. The famished will not receive their Bread. God Himself will not win that glory unless you consent to "mother Christ."

Angels with their annunciations "clean the doors of your perceptions." Everything now appears to you as it really is — kin to infinity — and you have found your center: God. Not only that, you have found the one word that will bring you His Word. You know now how to send Gabriel and his brothers back to God with His Christmas greeting returned in the only way He can accept it.

Fiat is the loving answer to God's "Will you?" It means "I will."

YOUR ONE WORD

There you have the mystery of love and the mystery of life along with the source and secret of happiness in very human words. Mary's *Fiat* will resound from the walls of our world so long as there are human hearts to love. For Gabriel will be sent from God with his "Fear not!" his "good tidings" and his "great joy" so long as there beats a human heart that can surrender itself to God. That is what the word means: full surrender, complete dedication — unconditional, eager, joyous giving of self. That giving is glorious in its garments of faith, hope, humility, generosity, and absolute trust. *Fiat* is a word of such disinterestedness that it speaks to God in somewhat the fashion the great mystic and poet of the Moslem Sufis, Rabi'a, spoke when he said: "God, if I worship Thee out of fear of hell, burn me in hell. And if I worship Thee only out of hope of Paradise, exclude me from Paradise. But if I worship Thee for Thine Own Sake, withhold not Thine Everlasting Beauty." The prayer is not that of a Christian and a Catholic — for fear of hell and hope of heaven have their place in reality. But it suggests the ideal toward which Christian and Catholic should strive — and which, at Christmastide, seems easily attainable; for when your world is filled with angels, when you cannot "stir a stone but you start a wing," then you grow to some semblance of your true greatness, and you want to love God the way Mary did when she said *Fiat*.

Gabriel and his brothers give you God's greeting and show you that it is God's will that His place in your life, His birth into your world, His embrace of your being is to be found in the *ordinary*. After Mary said *Fiat* Luke has a very short but very significant sentence: "With that, the Angel left her." Which means that once she had accepted God's Christmas greeting and returned it so generously and joyously, life resumed its *ordinary* external appearances. But oh, the extraordinary interior differences! God was in her. Yet she went about her usual daily tasks exteriorly the same as before. Even her husband-to-be did not know the change.

Do you see how God wants to keep your heart singing Christmas carols all the days of your life? As Mary did her everyday tasks, God was being formed in her, Christ was growing from moment to moment, and the Mass was being assured to the bankrupt race of sinful men. And in you — once

L
G-O-D
V
E

you have answered God with the flaming love cry of *Fiat* — the wheat, that will make the white Host, will gradually ripen into goldness, the grape, that will make the Wine, will swell unto purple sweetness; and you, like Mary, in your ordinary tasks, will allow Christ to form in you and make ready to say Mass.

If the sight of a shepherd shaping a crib changed all life for you, does not the whir of angel's wings and the whisper of his annunciation make the query: *Is life worth living?* seem blasphemy? Can there ever be question of the incalculable worth of human life and human living so long as one can say "Yes" to God? Life is a divine romance, or it is not living at all. But to make it that, one must hear the love call of God from the lips of Gabriel and send that angel back to God with the answer made by Mary.

That is the most important lesson in our prayerful study of this second letter: Gabriel brings you God's greeting, but he does not bring you God! *You* have to do that. You bring God to yourself. He awaits your *Fiat*. Once He hears that then He will do to you what He did to Mary — make you full of grace — render you blessed among women, and men, for He, the Lord, will be with you. Then you will have a joyful Christmas. And you will do what Mary did — make it possible for all the world to have the same. Say *Ecce ancilla* and you will immediately be able to add: *Ecce Agnus Dei.* Your Christmas carol can change from "The Lord is my Shepherd" to "God is my Lamb!"

Your world is filled with angels who have annunciations to make. Your soul should swell with hope. Now go on to the third letter in God's word. It enlivens *charity*.

L
G-O-D
V
E

28

THE VISITATION
BY PHILIPPE DE CHAMPAIGNE
MUSEE D'ART ET DI HISTOIRE, GENEVA, SWITZERLAND

A Virgin's Visit Gives God's First Syllable and Songs as Golden as the Sun

V, the third letter in God's word, tells of your Virgin-Mother and her first gracious act after conceiving God in her holy young body. Gabriel closed his annunciation to her with the news that her aged cousin Elizabeth was six months along with child. The Gospels then tell us that "Mary arose and went with haste into the hill country to a town of Juda" (Lk. 2:39).

That is the line which brings God closer to you than He has been up to now, and you will hear Him speak more clearly.

The awe that came over you as you looked at rain and wind and saw them as instruments in the hand of God, and as you looked on a lone shepherd who worked away intent on accomplishing something for himself yet actually sculpturing a crib to hold the Lamb of God, the reverent wonder which held you spellbound as you heard an angel make an announcement which told why all generations can call you blessed — these emotions leave you as you now quit Nazareth, hurry into the hill country, and visit with your Virgin-Mother the exultant Elizabeth.

You feel at home with these two happy women. Your whole heart and mind and being are at ease in what seems so natural and familiar — the joy of two expecting mothers who talk blissfully about the new life that throbs beneath their hearts. It seems normal, natural, and most human. But never was God nearer to you. You can all but reach out and touch the face of your Maker.

Here He is not the hidden God of that mighty yet mysterious Providence which blows the sun to flame, sets mountains smoking or stirs the ever moving sea to a mighty rush of waters. Nor is He that awe-inspiring Majesty which dwells in Light Inaccessible and sends angels to announce His will and His Word. No. Here He is only a heartthrob under the heart of a very young woman who has hastened into the hill country to help her aged cousin. Hence, when you look deep into this scene which is all sunshine and golden song your two arms reach out in a joy to your God who smiles at you through those deep wells of wonder and shining fountains of joy which are the eyes of His Mother — and yours.

God is near you! Nearer than ever before. Shepherds and sheep brought you the heat of the Burning Bush and the very voice of God. Angels with their annunciations had you look on that pillar of cloud which told you God was near and would speak as friend to friend. But the Virgin and her Visitation is something altogether different. Now you feel not only the warmth of God as He speaks from a bush aflame, not only the welcome intimacy of God as revealed by a column of cloud, but you will find the right hand of God across your eyes blinding you to the glory of His face, but allowing you to look after Him as that glory passes.

Do you remember when Moses went up the mountain to talk to God? The shepherd of the people of Israel voiced that hunger you feel in your heart when he begged God to grant him a sight of His glory. God replied: "All my splendor shall pass before thy eyes, and I will pronounce in thy presence my own name of Javé; . . . But my face, he said, thou canst not see; mortal man cannot see me and live to tell it. Then

L
G-O-D
V
E

30

he said, there is a place here, close by me, where thou mayst stand on a rock; there I will station thee, while my glory passes by, and cover thee with my right hand until I have gone past. So when I take my hand away thou shalt follow me with thy eyes . . ." (Exod. 33:18–23).*

Follow Him now with your eyes as you see Mary enter the three happiest months of her whole life. If our reckoning of time is right, and the Annunciation took place March the twenty-fifth, then April, May, and June were all sunshine and song for that young Maid you call your Blessed Mother. Joseph's brow had not furrowed with perplexity as yet. Simeon with his sight into things unborn was silently praying in the Temple. Herod's swords all slept in their sheathes. Mary had only the ecstasy of the all-adorable God who was but a pulse beat within her. These were months of bliss utterly unblemished. God, the Omnipotent, is within her; is hers, all hers; and He is safe. She is the Ark of the Covenant which holds the Manna for all mankind. She is the House of Gold whence God looks out on the world He made through the windows of her eyes. She is the Gate of Heaven through which God the Holy Ghost floods into the soul of Elizabeth; and the grace of Christ pours forth to free the unborn John from original sin, and sanctify him in his mother's womb. She is the Mother of Mercy and Fair Love; for God's mercy is His love — and she is the Mother of God. She is the Maid of the *Magnificat* who is this joy-filled atmosphere of Ain Karim, that town of Juda in the hill country, greets you not only with God's Christmas greeting but with God Himself, who will be both your *Christ* and your *Mass*. There is not a cloud in Mary's skies. The winds that brush her cheek are scented winds; for spring was generous with prophecies that were soon fulfilled, as perfumed petals unfolding. The air about Ain Karim is liquid with bird song; for He who placed sheen on the feathers that lift the

L
G-O-D
V
E

---

* Knox translation.

31

skylark into the dawn is here — and He must be praised. Do not your arms open out to that lovely little lady who is the Mother of God — and of you? Do you not feel the hand of God across your eyes?

Mary rose and went with all haste into the hill country. The reason for her hurry was certainly not to seek proof that God can do all things. She is all belief. But love must act; joy must manifest itself; goodness, give to others. Mary, all aglow with God, would hurry to help Elizabeth. But this haste is more than a revelation of the Immaculate Heart of your Mother. Remember the moment Mary had said *Fiat*, God became flesh within her. This haste to the hill country is God's haste to you!

The Incarnation was a coming in of God to flesh, but it was also and more especially a going out of God to men. And that is why Mary hurries to the hills. Your God spurs her on; for He would greet you with the sunshine and song of the Visitation. God always takes the initiative. Action which befits men and women who have been redeemed, namely super-natural action, is always divine in origin; your human response and the total effect always follows on God's lead. God is first to greet you. You can only return His greeting. God sent Gabriel to Mary to give her a chance to choose Him for her Child, but only after He had first chosen her as His Mother. And God loved you long, long aeons before you could begin to love Him. Now He is hurrying into the hill country to seek you and set this pattern for all His actions with men, before any men can begin to seek Him. This Visitation of Mary to Elizabeth is truly a going out of God. The Lamb who is the Good Shepherd is seeking His sheep.

You have had the parable of the Prodigal Son recalled to your mind. It is a story true in its symbolism of your God who is your forgiving Father. But now as Mary hurries from Naza-reth, and toils those eighty miles to "The Vineyard Spring" — which is what Ain Karim means — you see how much more beautiful is the parable of the Good Shepherd; and how much truer to the plan and action of your God. The Prodigal entered into himself when utterly destitute, and resolved to return to his waiting and watchful father. Of course the point of the parable is the forgivingness of that Father, who is your God. But in the story of the Good Shepherd, it is not the stray sheep that makes the initial move. It is the Shepherd who leaves the ninety-nine who are safe and hurries after the one who is lost. Christmas tells you that parable by its application. God comes after *you!* And in the Visitation you see how impatient God was to find you. He is but a tiny creature in the womb; yet he must act the Good Shepherd and seek out His sheep. He must sanctify. He must begin scattering the gold of His yet unsaid Christ-Mass. The first recipient, after Mary, will be that child in the aged Elizabeth's womb, the one who will win for himself the name of Baptist, and be that "Angel which goes before the face of God."

Note Mary's place in God's plan for you: Christ, your Good Shepherd, will find you only if Mary, His Mother, leads the way. It is not that Omnipotence needs aid, nor that the Creator depends on His creature, but only that He who is Almighty may do great things in you that His approach is as tender as the smile on Mary's youthful face. His coming to you is as gentle as her soft-spoken greeting of "Peace be to you!" But the effects of her greeting will be similar to what happened when she entered Zachary's home and said "Peace be to you" to Elizabeth. You will be filled with God. You will say your "Hail Mary" and feel the joy of sanctity leap within you. God comes to you through Mary. Such is His eternal decree. And it is another proof that God does things in reverse. Who would ever think that the all-strong God would be so dependent on a weak woman? Who would ever suppose that she who had just conceived God the Son through God the Holy Ghost would rise up and hurry to her who had conceived only a man through the action of a man? Who would ever dream that the

MARY'S
PLACE IN
YOUR LIFE

L
G-O-D
V
E

33

Mother of the Forerunner would be sought out by the Mother of the Messias?

And she is the first to speak. As she crossed the threshold there fell from her lips the lovely Jewish greeting of "Peace be to you." Was it ever spoken before or since with so much meaning and so much truth? Under her Immaculate Heart was beating the heart of the Prince of Peace, at whose birth heaven would burst with a song of peace to men of good will, after whose Resurrection this greeting of peace would fall from glorified lips.

Mary stands at the threshold of your soul. Before removing her veil or mantle she will say "Peace be to you!" If you are like Elizabeth, wonders will be multiplied. For Christ will have found His stray. Grace will go out to sanctify. The "Hail Mary" will receive increase of words in praise of the Word and the all-lovable Mother of the Word.

That is what happened that golden day at Ain Karim. Gabriel was the first of the angelic world to hail Mary as "full of grace," and tell her that the Lord was with her; Elizabeth was the first of humankind to continue the prayer with "Blessed art thou among women, and blessed is the fruit of thy womb." You name the Fruit of her womb as "Jesus" and complete the first half of that sweetest of prayers called "Hail Mary." For fifteen centuries that was all of it. The salutation of the angel at Nazareth and the exultant cry of the woman at Ain Karim echoed and re-echoed throughout the then known world. Five hundred years ago Holy Mother Church added the second half naming Mary "Mother of God," which is but a clarification of Gabriel's message and Elizabeth's cry. But then the Church in her wisdom added a plea for us sinners "now and at the hour of our death," completing Mary's Motherhoods, and allowing you to do what Gabriel could not do, and what was as yet impossible to Elizabeth — name Mary as Co-Redemptress with Him who is your Christ-Mass. The Annunciation and the Visitation are like Christmas itself — facts more than feasts,

L
G-O-D
V
E

34

perpetual rather than passing, of hourly occurrence and momentary commemoration. Thrice at the end of Mass the priest says Hail Mary. And every hour of the Divine Office God's ministers say Hail Mary. All the day long and into the darkness of the night, every night, hundreds of millions of the faithful say what Gabriel and Elizabeth said to Mary, then add what Mother Church would have us ask of her. Mary's prophecy uttered that day at Ain Karim as she hymned her *Magnificat* — that Christmas carol of Christ's own Mother — is being fulfilled by you and hundreds of millions like you. All generations have, all generations will, the present generations do call her blessed!

But Elizabeth's loud cry after Mary's greeting and her first words tell you that God had told her what you have been learning, namely, that the leap of joy within her which was her son, was due to Mary's coming with Christ. A mother, especially one who had so miraculously conceived as Elizabeth, would normally be so absorbed in her child that she would talk of nothing else. The leap John made within her should have her thinking of nothing else. Yet she greets Mary first and names her blessed among women, then goes on to talk, not of her own, but of Mary's Child, and names Him "Blessed"; it is only in third place that she makes any mention of her own and of his joy. That is the God-consciousness you must have as Mary visits you and says: "Peace be to you!" — which is only God's latest way of phrasing His Christmas greetings to you. But it is a fuller revelation of what Christmas means; for it speaks clearly of that gift of all gifts which you name "grace."

John the Baptist leaped for joy. His mother tells you that. But it is God's theologians who tell you why he leaped with such joy. He had been baptized, as it were, by Mary's breath. The shackles of original sin fell from his soul. He received a new, a higher, a holy life. Grace went into him. God, through Mary, had lifted His Precursor, while still in his

THE GIFT
OF GIFTS

35

mother's womb, to the dazzling height of supernatural vitality. Do you know that when Christ said of Himself, "I came that they might have life, and have it more abundantly," He was talking of this higher life? Now you can realize that this utterly unattainable height, this Gift beyond every mortal's reach, this unbelievable generosity of God is nothing less than a share in His own divine Life. It is through His Christ and that Christ's Mass that you can live above nature, that you can breathe the rarified atmosphere Sanctity itself lives in. Mary brings that air to you as she stands on your threshold and says: "Peace be to you." And the Virgin is ever making Visitations to you.

Must you not imitate Elizabeth and cry aloud: "Whence is this to me?" Whence is it that God — the only all-sufficient, the only self-sufficient, the one and only ineffable Absolute — should come to *you?* Whence is it that He should have the splendor of His dazzling Godhead shine out on you from a girl's eyes that are alight with the glory which is God? Whence is it that He whose word is might, should speak to you through this winsome girl from Nazareth?

There is an answer, an all-satisfying answer. But it rises from the logic of the heart, and never from that of the intellect alone. You have heard it often already, but you can never hear it often enough. It is: *Love does such things.*

That is the only answer. It is not only philosophic, it is theologic — that logic of God, who is Love. By this time, after seeing so much of shepherds and sheep, angels and annunciations, the Virgin and her Visitation, you should be ready to take God at His word when He says: "I have loved *you* with an everlasting love." Think of all the thought, time, and attention He had to give so that you could be called a child of Mary, and have your Mother standing now on the threshold of your soul laden with grace and anxious to give *Him* to you! You have seen that it took aeons to shape the cave in Bethlehem's chalk hills. But have you ever thought of all the concern it cost God that Bethlehem be in the land of Juda, that Jesse's root be sunk in the soil of the little town, and that David should be watching flocks there when Samuel came with the oils for Israel's second and greatest King? Men, you know, are not puppets who dance to the pull of the strings in the hands of God. They are free agents, with a freedom like unto God's own freedom. Secondary causes, of course, but real causes. Hence, if every word that God had uttered through the mouths of Patriarch and Prophet concerning His only Word, was to be fulfilled before the fullness of time had come, He had to be on the alert, as it were, as history unrolled and tribes fought over the land that was to be the Promised Land. He had to watch closely after the Chosen People had crossed the Jordan and the battlements of Jericho had been blown down by the blasts of trumpets; He had to listen to Josue and have His sun and moon stand still that His men might pursue the Amorrites; He had to be patient as countless kings, singly and in alliances, were conquered and killed by the Israelites; then He had to be watchfulness itself as the Tribes portioned out the Promised Land by lot. For Bethlehem had to be within the confines of that territory which fell to the lot of Juda. Then when the lovely Ruth won the heart of Booz, God had to exert His influence to see that Obed was born in Bethlehem and that there he would father Jesse, the man who was to have seven stalwart sons before he begot the immortal David. God was thinking of His only Son and His ancestors for centuries before that shepherd you have seen began to chip away that stone which would be Christ's crib — and during all that time God was thinking of *you*.

Twelve centuries before the birth of Christ, God was arranging things in such a manner that you, twenty centuries after that birth, might be singing as one of your sweetest Christmas carols "O Little Town of Bethlehem," and telling the charming truth that "amid the cold of winter there came

37

L
G-O-D
V
E

a floweret" from the stem of Jesse. That carol credits Isaias with foretelling your Christmas rose, but one of the most winsome of the prophecies about your Christ is that of Micheas. God had him speak it seven hundred years before Mary and Joseph headed toward David's city to answer Augustus' imperial edict about enrollment. The original differs from what you have in the Gospels, spoken at the time the Magi were lost in Jerusalem because the star had faded. Matthew reads: "And thou, Bethlehem, of the land of Juda, art by no means least among the princes of Juda . . ." (Mt. 2:6). But Micheas said the opposite. He said: "Thou *art* the least . . ." His statement about the birth of Christ reads like a song. Well might it be a Christmas carol.

> And thou, Bethlehem of Ephrata, art a little one among the thousands of Juda: out of thee shall he come forth unto me that is to be the Ruler in Israel: and his going forth is from the beginning, from the days of eternity (Mich. 5:1).

From the days of eternity God was thinking of Bethlehem — and of you! Believe Him when He says "I have loved thee with an everlasting love." Then look into your own life's history and you will see that in every great act it was God who took the initiative, just as this Second Joyful Mystery of your Rosary proves. How did you come to be elevated to a share in that life which caused the unborn Baptist to leap with joy? How did you come to be a Child of Mary, that Immaculate Maid who is Spouse of the Holy Ghost and who brings that Spirit of Love with her on her every Visitation? How did you come to be kin to Him who is God's only Son and Mary's first-born Child? How did you come to be heir with rightful claim on God and His heaven? You can reply: "Love does such things! — and God is Love." Is not the correct answer contained in the one word God speaks to you as Christmas greeting? Beyond all doubt He has loved you with an everlasting love; and He always takes the initiative.

L
G-O-D
V
E

38

You can hear Mary singing this truth as she replies to Elizabeth's greeting with her *Magnificat*. That prayer of praise and gratitude to God merits your study at Christmastide. It tells you so much about your God and that lovely Lady you call your Mother. It will not only kindle your faith, it will inflame your hope, and your charity. Read it as the Kleist-Lilly translation has it and you will capture more of its sweetness and truth. Elizabeth had just said: "As the sound of your greeting fell on my ears, the babe in my womb leaped for joy! Happy is she who believed that what was told her on behalf of the Lord would be fulfilled." Elizabeth is referring to the Annunciation and the Incarnation, though as yet Mary has told her nothing of what happened at Nazareth. But when her aged cousin says that Mary is happy because she had believed, the girl breaks forth:

> My soul extols the Lord;
> and my spirit leaps for joy in God my Saviour.

> How graciously he looked upon his lowly maid!
> Oh, behold, from this hour onward
> age after age will call me blessed!

> How sublime is what he has done for me —
> the Mighty One, whose name is "Holy"! (Lk. 1:46–49.)

That is the first third of Mary's song, and it is well to ponder on what she sings. It is of the might and the mercy of God. That it is a spontaneous, extempore surging of her soul is evident from the echoing she does of Elizabeth. This aged woman had named her young cousin "Mother of my Lord"; Mary echoes those words in "My soul extols the Lord." Elizabeth had said John "leaped for joy"; Mary repeats the identical words as she tells that her "spirit leaps for joy in God my Saviour." The mother of the Baptist had called Mary "blessed among women"; the Virgin Mother snatches at the phrase and molds it into a prophecy: "Oh, behold, from this hour onward age after age will call me blessed!"

L
G-O-D
V
E

39

Extempore it certainly is, yet such sublimity of thought and majesty of expression tells that Elizabeth's words had sent the Maiden-Mother into an ecstasy of awe and adoration of the infinite glories of God. She sees herself against a background of eternal light and infinite power and she does what you must ever do. She sings: "Magnificat anima mea *Dominum.*" She extols *the Lord.* She praises God. That is why she was made. That is why you were made.

But look closely at her second line and you will hear her singing about Christmas; you will suddenly realize that the *Magnificat* is Mary's Christmas carol; it is her cradle song for God who is her Baby! Note that Mary calls God her Saviour. In the New Testament that title is reserved to Christ. In the Old Testament it is found frequently enough, but seldom, if ever, with the personal stress Mary places on it here. To catch what she actually sang you will have to render the line: "my spirit leaps for joy in God *my Jesus.*" That name has been ringing in her blood ever since Gabriel spoke it. Mary is all mother as she sings. She is extoling God, it is true; yet she is crooning a lullaby to that God who is already in the cradle He placed under her heart when He made her all pure at the moment of her conception. Since you know the sweetest songs our earth ever hears are those a mother croons to her child, do not wonder at the sweetness of the *Magnificat;* love rather your singing Mother.

Do you not hear some echo of your own Christmas carol: "God is my Shepherd; and nothing do I want"? (Ps. 22.) You, too, are singing of the might and the mercy of God as you tell all He does for you in His ever kind Providence. But then, like Mary, you end with praise of His Holy Name. The cycle is thus completed; that cycle you see in all creation, wherein everything that comes out from God somehow or other goes back to Him. God graces and gifts you and Mary; both of you praise Him for it; and thus give back the glory He showed forth in giving to you. That is prayer in purest

L
G-O-D
V
E

40

form; that is life at highest pitch; that is health of mind and happiness of heart; that is being in harmony with your Maker, and with all that He has made.

Once Mary had sung of God's mercy and might shown in her own regard, she thought of you. Not individually, as God has been thinking of you from all eternity, but in a general, inclusive way. Everyone born of woman is named in the lines:

> From age to age he visits those
> who worship him in reverence.

> His arm achieves the mastery:
> he routs the haughty and proud of heart;
> he puts down princes from their thrones,
> and exalts the lowly;

> he fills the hungry with blessings,
> and sends away the rich with empty hands (Lk. 1:50–53).*

Misericordia is the Latin equivalent for the term Mary used. You render it in English as "mercy." But that is a translation that does not really translate. It is too weak a word for that all-powerful attribute of God. His mercy is that phase of His love which sets His omnipotence to work. Hence His mercy is His might, and His mercy and might only other aspects of His love. That is why you must conceive this *Misericordia* of which Mary sings as that which makes Omnipotence tender and true; which sets the Shepherd in God Almighty earnestly seeking His strays; which has the Maker of men searching out a Mother that He may become Man and find us all! It was God's mercy which hollowed out Bethlehem's Cave, shaped Bethlehem's Crib, sent Gabriel to find that Maid who would Mother Bethlehem's Babe — for *you.* There is where you see the mercy and might of God — and your two arms go out to Him! Power that is Omnipotence, pardon that is infinite, leniency and love that are God, look out at you from the tender eyes of this Maid who sings

L
G-O-D
V
E

---

* Kleist-Lilly translation.

Magnificat at this moment of Visitation. They will look out at you and at all men at Christmas from the winsome eyes of a Child at Bethlehem. Oh, the might and the mercy of God that gave you Mary and her Son. *Magnificat* is your song. Sing it with all your soul. Mary sings of God's faithfulness and that is what can fill you to brimming over with a Faith that will never know hesitation or doubt. God keeps His word. Listen to Mary singing this truth:

> He has taken by the hand his servant Israel,
> and mercifully kept his faith
> — as he had promised our father —
> with Abraham and his posterity
> forever and evermore. (Lk. 1:54–55.)*

GOD IS FAITHFUL

This is the twentieth century after the birth of Christ. Mary sang her *Magnificat* just twenty centuries after God had sworn to Abraham. What she said of God then, you can sing of Him now. He takes you by the hand today just as tenderly and as truly as He took Israel then. He does it "in Christ Jesus" — in Him who is your Christ-Mass! Does not this reference to Abraham, who is your spiritual father in the Faith, show you that Christ was ever in God's mind? You recall the moment so tense with drama when the faith-filled patriarch raised the knife to slay his only son, Isaac. It was a symbol of another drama-filled moment when a Father would not stay the hand which was raised, and He who was symbolized by Isaac — the only Son of God — would die. A ram was substituted for Isaac, but for the Lamb of God there would be no substitute; for He was already substituting for you. Forty centuries ago God was thinking of you and preparing your Christ-Mass as "The Angel of the Lord called to Abraham a second time from heaven." Then came God's solemn word: "By my own self have I sworn, saith the Lord: because thou hast done this thing, and hast

L
G-O-D
V
E

---

* Kleist-Lilly translation.

42

not spared thy only begotten son for my sake: I will bless thee . . . and in thy seed shall all the nations of the earth be blessed, because thou hast obeyed my voice" (Gen. 22:15-18). Mary is standing singing her *Magnificat* with that Seed, which was to bless all nations, already growing within her. God is faithful — you can be full of faith.

Mary, of course, had before her in her cousin Elizabeth proof that God is to be taken at His word. To find this aged woman heavy with her first child was miracle enough to set souls far less God-conscious than Mary's singing the praises of God. To have Elizabeth cry out loudly and name the greater miracle that had happened to Mary, commanded like praise. That John leaped for joy and his mother prophesied were signs of God's presence in the air of Ain Karim. But have you any less evidence of God's presence or of His fidelity?

How is it that the entire world is Christian for at least one day every year — Christmas Day? Even atheists commemorate the birthday of God. Communists date their every paper and publication from the time Mary said *Fiat* and God took flesh. Each time you hear a Christmas greeting, you hear someone saying that God is faithful! If you need miraculous proof, look at the Catholic Church. There you see not only God's mercy but His might. All the hate of the Caesars, ancient and modern, have been hurled at her; she goes on loving. The concentrated might of empires has been turned on her again and again, the empires fall and fade away; she goes on growing. Monarchs rally all their resources to kill her. The monarchs, one after another, die; she lives on. The Circus Maximus of Imperial Rome is dust; and over it the Dome of St. Peters is often set ablaze with lights to tell that some new saint has joined those who were made human torches in Nero's Gardens. The crumbling Colosseum, when contrasted with the solidity of the Vatican buildings, ought to tell you that God is faithful and that you can be full of faith. He

L
G-O-D
V
E

promised to be with His Church all days. He swore that the very Gates of Hell would not prevail against her.

But the miracle is evident not only in Rome. Go to Paris and enter the Church of Notre Dame. Kneel before the high altar and ask yourself where are the Dantons, the Robespierres, the French Revolutionists and their Goddess of Reason whom they so sacrilegiously set upon that altar? Mary's Son is there, and there Christ's Mass is daily offered. Look south to Mexico. Calles is dead and well-nigh forgotten. Christ is cheered hourly. He lives more vigorously in the hearts of His people, for they have known the hunger for God which can be appeased here on earth only by the Bread that came down from heaven when Mary said *Fiat*.

Once you course through history and see as Mary saw, you will sing *Magnificat* as Mary sang it; for you will know that God is faithful and that His mercy and might are never failing. You are surrounded by miracle and every day hear prophecy fulfilled when you hear a "Hail Mary" said or the Angelus bell being tolled. You have your proofs more numerous than Mary had, and, in their own way, more miraculous. Your faith should leap as joyously as did the Baptist, and your soul should ever be singing; for you should ever be saying:

> My soul extols the Lord;
> and my spirit leaps for joy *in God my Saviour*. . . .
> How sublime is what he has done *for me* —
> the Mighty One, whose name is "Holy"! . . .
> he has taken by the hand his servant . . .
> and mercifully kept his faith. . . . (Lk. 1:46–54.)*

THE DUMB
SPEAKS

But the singing is not ended yet, nor is God's greeting coming to you only from Mary. For six months a priest of God has been dumb. As Mary enters his house it is his joy-filled wife who has to do all the talking. For three months more this priest will be silent; but in that silence he will be

---

* Kleist-Lilly translation. Emphasis added.

44

able to observe the might and the mercy of God as it moves about his home in the persons of Mary and Elizabeth and the Sons they hold beneath their hearts. He had doubted God's word as it came to him from the lips of Gabriel. For that doubt his own lips were sealed. For nine months he watched and saw the word of God fulfilled before his eyes. It is no wonder, then, that when God in His mercy unsealed Zachary's lips, the old man should give vent to that song we call the *Benedictus*. Its first lines, like those of Mary's song, speak of Christmas: hence they hold God's greeting to you.

Blessed be the Lord, the God of Israel!

He has visited his people
and brought about its redemption.

There you have another Christmas carol. It takes you to Bethlehem as you hear:

He has raised for us a stronghold of salvation
in the house of David his servant . . .

And it takes you back through that long line of prophets who foretold God's faithfulness, as Zachary continues:

and redeemed the promise he made
through the mouth of his holy prophets of old . . .
to deal in mercy with our fathers
and be mindful of his holy covenant,
of the oath he had sworn to our father Abraham,
that he would enable us
. . . .
to worship him without fear
in holiness and observance of the Law,
in his presence, all our days. (Lk. 1:68–75.)*

Zachary, like Mary, says that God is faithful.
As were those of Elizabeth, these opening words of Zachary are the opposite to what you would normally expect. His son

L
G-O-D
V
E

---

* Kleist-Lilly translation.

has been born and just named, yet the burden of his song is about the unborn Son of Mary whose name is so holy and so laden with meaning that the aged priest can only paraphrase it and sing a song that reaches back through the ages to the beginning of time, then onward through unborn countless centuries to Time's last moment, as it tells of God's might and mercy and His unwavering faithfulness.

But that is only proper, as Zachary, under guidance of the Holy Ghost, well knows; for while his son is to be "Prophet of the Most High," he will be but the Voice of that Word who is the Most High, and who will fulfill all prophecies. The loosed tongue of the old priest names his boy as Forerunner of God, but dares not name the name of Mary's Son with anything less than Salvation and Redemption. He knows his son will be the Lamp, but Mary's Son will be the Light. So he sings:

> Thanks be to the merciful heart of our God!
> A dawning Light from on high will visit us
> to shine upon those who sit in darkness
> and in the shadowland of death,
> and guide our feet into the path of peace. (Lk. 1:78–79.)*

Those lines are a Christmas carol telling you truths about your God which may well serve to carry you from the blissful air of Ain Karim, which was so filled with sunshine and song, to the sacred silence of Bethlehem. You go from Mary's happiest days and some of her holiest hours to the moment of her highest bliss — the moment you call *Christmas*.

---

* Kleist-Lilly translation.

L
G-O-D
V
E

THE NATIVITY
BY FEDERIGO BAROCCIO
PRADO MUSEUM, MADRID, SPAIN

His Nativity and His Nameday
Give You God's Word

I, the next letter you meet in your spelling, gives you God's greeting in *person!* You have seen it often, of course, in "IHS," the monogram for the name "Jesus."

Shepherds and sheep have spoken to you, and as you listened you must have heard at least a whisper of that voice which alone can say, and which alone says incessantly: "I have loved thee with an everlasting love." As angels made annunciations you must have learned in some dim fashion that you have lived long, long aeons before you were born, and that all during that measureless time you were loved with a special love. Just now a Virgin by her Visitation gave you such golden songs that your very spirit leaped within you at the joyous realization that Love Incarnate was looking out at you through the grace-filled eyes of Mary and the Light of the World was beginning to rise in a new way over your world. But now God is done with men and angels, even with His Maiden-Mother, as His mouthpieces. No longer need you listen for His voice as it comes in wind and rain; no longer look to special men or chosen angel; now not even to His Mother. He loves you so much that He must greet you in person! His voice was not enough. He gives you His *Word!*

No Bush is Burning. No column of cloud stands still. The right hand of God itself is taken away, and you do what Moses

47

never did. He saw the glory of God only after it had passed. You look on the God of Glory present in person before you.

"I" stands for the Nativity of your God Incarnate and for the name above all names that was given Him by His Father before He was conceived in His Mother's womb. It brings you to the birth and to that ceremony which foreshadowed baptism; for it gives you those holydays which are world-wide holidays: Christmas and New Year's.

They are familiar feasts, but they hold facts that are not nearly familiar enough to the minds and hearts of millions. So for a few moments blind your eyes to everyone and everything but the Child; stop your ears to every sound save that of the Word; blot out of existence by a blazing act of your will your entire world and everything in it except your God. He is speaking to you personally and in Person! Mary has just brought Him forth in that cave you saw hollowed out of the hills by God Himself. She has wrapped Him in swaddling clothes and laid Him in that manger you saw being chipped out of chalk by an unknown shepherd that he might have a hollow that would hold fodder for his sheep. He is the Child Mary conceived by the Holy Ghost when she sent Gabriel back to God with her *Fiat*. He is what Elizabeth called the blessed fruit of Mary's womb and whose name Mary gave as "Holy." He is the Child Zachary called Salvation. He is your God. . . . But the peoples of the Western World and especially those of northern climes have heaped so much sentiment on the Babe that often there is no room for the adoration due to God. Christmas has become sheer poetry and the Second Person of the all-holy Trinity teaches His deep and sublimely spiritual doctrine to inattentive pupils.

GOD SPEAKS
TO YOU

God speaks! Fail to be alive to that fact and you will never really live. As Romano Guardini has so pithily stated it: "The Everlasting, God and His Kingdom, speak constantly to man; were it otherwise, life would be senseless." As you spell out the one word with which God greets you, do not think for

48

a moment that you are dealing with anything but fact. Empty fancy has no place in your soul when you are face to face with your God. This spelling out is a sacred, serious, soul-searing experience; it is the attuning of your whole being to Him who *is;* it is tossing aside the trifles of time to lay a firm grasp on rigid reality, on eternal verity. It is, in all truth, touching the untouchable God.

God speaks — and He speaks to you incessantly. Everything in nature is a mouthpiece through which the Creator speaks. David, as a shepherd boy, looked up to the stars one night and heard them as we all should hear them — singing as the Christmas angels sang. Then he himself burst into this song: *Coeli enarrant gloriam Dei* — "the Heavens proclaim the glory of God." St. Paul of the Cross used to shake his stick at the fields and the flowers and beg them to hush, so loudly did they speak to him of God or, better, so clearly did God speak to him through them. Let this thousand-tongued language of God sound in your soul every hour of the day, and night. God is everywhere and though we are right in naming Him a hidden God, we can never be right if we name Him a silent God.

Though God speaks to you incessantly through nature, there is a more intimate communication going on between you and your God that is just as incessant. Down deep in you is what mystics speak of as "the high point of the soul." It is really the ground of your substantial self. There the God who made you sustains you. There, it may well be imagined, that gift named sanctifying grace inheres. There the Trinity make its abode as Christ promised. It is there those assurances arise that all is well, those stirrings of the nobler part of you, those promptings to be and to do better than you have ever been or done. It is there that many believe God speaks incessantly to each and every human being, whether each listens or not. For one can turn the inner ear away from God. One can become harder and harder of hearing, until one is totally

L
G-O-D
V
E

49

deaf. On the other hand you can make your ear so keen that God need never more than whisper to you. Then not only will you see God everywhere, but you will hear His voice in everything, and most especially in those ever tone-true stirrings of your conscience. That is what carries God's messages to you no matter where be the place of His dwelling within you and the point of converse.

But the world within you and the world without you are often very noisy worlds. God knew, and yet knows, that. That is why He spoke through others. Already you have heard Him speaking for forty centuries as you listened to Him take oath by Himself to bless Abraham, his seed, and all nations through him. That speech of God and mention of seed, must have awakened echoes of that first intimation of Christmas given by Him in the Garden. So from the beginning of time you have heard God speaking to you. And the sole topic of conversation has been His Word! Now you hear the Word.

LISTEN TO THE WORD

There is only one posture in which to receive the Word and that is on your knees. Let David speak to you before His Son does. Let the Shepherd-King give wise advice before the Lamb of God and the King of kings utters a sound. Let this one who was called a "man after God's own Heart" look at you with burningly serious eyes and say: "Today, if you hear His Voice, harden not your heart" (Ps. 94).

The first thing the Word says to you is: "Kindly remember I am Wisdom."

That request is necessary. For well-meaning persons, pious souls, have inculcated into the young the thought that they should sympathize with the Babe of Bethlehem, feel sorry that He had no better bed than the manger, no better clothes than swaddling bands, no better home than the cattle cave, no better company than the traditional ox and ass. Jesus has to say: "Kindly remember I am Wisdom." You need to be shocked into the realization that deliberately and with clarity

L
G-O-D
V
E

of foresight and forethought, He very definitely chose this cave, this crib, these bands and these beasts, if beasts were there. Sympathy is out of place. There is room only for docility. Jesus is speaking to you through these accompaniments of His birth. He, the Word, knew and knows that actions speak louder even than His words. So He would teach you by His careful choice what you are to choose if you will be wise with His wisdom.

When choosing His Mother He was most select. He took the Maid who had been dowered by heaven as no one before or since. He would have the Peerless Woman, the Immaculate Conception, the girl who was full of grace, the impeccable one. You see the propriety of such a choice. It was only befitting that the Mother of the infinite God should border on the Infinite. Do you think for a moment that He who was so choice about the place in which He was to be conceived was any whit less delicate about His choice of the place in which He would be born?

According to St. Matthew, Jesus' first sermon was the Sermon on the Mount, in which He pronounced the Beatitudes. But can you not hear Him in His manger saying to you "Blessed are the poor in spirit"? Here is His first sermon. All the others were but reiteration and amplification. God is speaking in that little bundle of flesh Mary has wrapped in swaddling clothes. God is speaking from the pulpit of a cattle crib. God is speaking of values. It is a sharper sermon than the Sermon on the Mount, though it proclaims the same Beatitudes. It is sharper, because actions speak louder than words. The God of all wealth and wisdom beggared Himself of everything but a baby's body to teach you real worth.

This is what St. Bernard heard God saying from the crib: "It was not for earthly honor that the 'Almighty Word leapt down from heaven from His royal throne,' where 'length of days is in His Right Hand and in His Left Hand riches and glory.' He possessed from everlasting an inexhaustible store

L
G-O-D
V
E

51

of all such things in heaven. One treasure, however, He could not find there, namely, the *treasure of poverty* — of which there was on earth an abundance and even a superabundance, although man had no suspicion of its *worth*. It was for this, therefore, that the Son of God came down from His throne on high: to choose it for Himself, and by His choice *to teach us its value*." (1st Sermon for Christmas Eve. Emphasis added.)

You begin to see where your sympathy should go: not to the newborn Infant who lies awake in poverty, but to the adult world that sleeps in its riches. Herod was wealthy with the Throne of David — he was asleep when the Heir to that throne was born. The high priests, whose duty it was to watch over the House of the Father, were deep in slumber when the Son of the Father came. The Scribes, rich in learning, the men who knew the time and the place the Saviour was to be born, slept when Mary brought the Messias forth. The City of Jerusalem, steeped in the riches of holiness from the time David founded it as a capitol for the nation, and which had become the religious center of the people, went on sleeping when the King of that nation and people appeared. The whole land of Juda and of the people of God, rich with the wealth of His countless blessings, was fast asleep when their God was laid in a manger. Even from the crib you can hear that dread pronouncement from the lips of God: "Woe to the rich!"

GOD'S GIFT
TO YOU

L
G-O-D
V
E

Miss the point that the Child in the manger is God and you have missed the whole point of Christmas. This is not the greatest Feast of the year by any means. The Annunciation with the Incarnation is far superior in mysteries and miracles. The Feast of Easter is rightly named "the solemnity of solemnities." And think of Pentecost! But this is the most popular and best loved Feast; for it really is the Feast of Love and is best summed up in that glorious line: "God so loved the world that He gave His only-begotten Son." But do not lay all stress on the word "love." "God" is the subject

52

of that sentence and God is the object; and "give" is the verb. Fail to grasp the fact that God the Father, who brought forth the Son before the Morning Star ever shone, now gives you that Son; fail to grasp the eternal birth of this only Son, and the birth in the manger is meaningless.

That danger is so real that God cries out through the liturgy in the Midnight Mass. Our Holy Mother the Church, through whom God speaks, who is the "pillar and ground of truth," in tones deep with majesty, but mellow with awe and love, tells us in the Midnight Mass of the three births of Christ. As the Sacred Ministers approach the altar to begin the Sacrifice you hear the voice of God the Father as He says to the Son: *Filius meus es tu; ego hodie genui te* – "Thou art my Son; this day have I begotten thee." After the Epistle the same God will again speak out and say: *Ex utero ante Luciferum genui te* – "I begot thee from my bosom before the Morning Star." It is the eternal birth of God the Son that God the Father and Holy Mother Church recalls to your mind as you assist at Midnight Mass to commemorate His temporal birth at Bethlehem.

With a wisdom born of God the liturgy takes you back to the night of eternity to orientate you properly for the splendor of the "Holy Night when God was born." She ushers you into that dark which held only God; for before any dawn broke or any star shone God was – and in Him was His Word, and it is that Word which was made Flesh. Listen to Mother Church wrestling with words in order to give exact expression to this deep mystery and all-splendid truth. In the Creed you sing at Mass she has you say: ". . . I believe in Jesus Christ, only begotten Son of God, born of the Father before all ages; God of God, Light of Light, true God of true God; begotten not made, of the same substance as the Father, by whom all things were made. . . ."

Now you can look at the Child in the manger and hear eternal Wisdom speak; for you know that in Him are hidden

L
G-O-D
V
E

all the treasures of wisdom and knowledge; "for in Him dwelleth all the fullness of the Godhead corporeally" (Col. 2:9).

Before you become absorbed in the loveliness of the Child in the manger, Holy Mother Church speaks to you in the Epistle about the final coming of Christ; for she would have you learn the real secret of joy and initiate you into the true cause of merriment on Christmas Day. She wants you to hear God speaking to you. So she has St. Paul addressing you as "Dearly beloved"—and you are that not only to Paul, but to Mother Church, and Mother Mary, and Jesus in the crib, and to God the Father, who generated Him before all time, and to God the Holy Ghost who overshadowed Mary that God the Son might know a birth in the flesh. It is this Triune God and your two loving Mothers who speak in this Epistle, saying: "Dearly beloved, the grace of God, which is the means of salvation for all men, has made its appearance and instructed us to reject irreligion and worldly lusts and to live prudent, just, and religious lives in this world, while we await the realization of our blessed hope, *the brilliant coming of our great God and Savior, Jesus Christ*. He gave Himself for us, to redeem us from every kind of iniquity, and cleanse a people for his very own, zealous for good deeds" (Tit. 2:11–14).*

Now you can hear the Babe saying: "I am the Lord, thy God. I made thee. I have come to redeem thee. I shall be thy Judge."

Does the message of the crib become clearer? The Lamb of God is your Good Shepherd. He has come seeking you, His stray sheep. He has come to show you the way to happiness. "I am the Way," He will yet say. Then add: "I am the Truth, and the Life!" He is speaking eternal truths from His crib that will show you the way to eternal life. Look and listen!

There have been men who have really merited the name of

L
G-O-D
V
E

---

* Kleist-Lilly translation. Emphasis added.

"wise." But there had never before been a man who could rightly be called "Wisdom." Look at Wisdom in swaddling bands. Men may choose where they will live, but no man ever before has chosen where he would be born. Look at the One who chose to be born in a cave. He is Wisdom and infinitely free will. Men may gift their mothers all during life. But never before was there a Child who graced His Mother as this Child has done long before His birth. Now ask yourself if men were allowed to choose their parents, the time, place, and circumstances of their births, how many would have chosen a peasant girl not out of her teens, a cattle shed, midnight, with no one but a poor carpenter and perhaps a beast or two near?

God is speaking. He is telling you how to be *truly* merry at Christmas; for His one Word, which is His greeting and His gift, is also your goal! Hence the cave, the crib, the darkness of the night, the cold of winter, and the deliberate choice to be the Son of a poor peasant girl from a despised city, of a despised province, of a despised people, speak with divine eloquence about the way to attain to God and eternal happiness. For when God wishes you to be merry it is not for a day, not for a time, but for an eternity; and God, being God, makes no idle wishes, nor does He waste divine words! So from His manger, in plainest language, He is saying that poverty, lowliness, humble station in life, lack of social prestige, discomfort, pain, and privation are not evil things. He is saying "Beware of the wisdom of the world!"

What modern man, what worldling would have made the choices eternal Wisdom made? But Jesus Christ can neither deceive nor be deceived. Therefore the way to your goal, the way to real happiness, the way to a Merry Christmas in time and for eternity is not the way of the world.

Jesus is saying: "My child, my loved one, you can have treasure which thieves cannot steal, rust corrode, or moth

YOUR
WAY TO
HAPPINESS

L
G-O-D
V
E

consume, without having any of the riches or wealth of this world. You can be great with a greatness that is real, without holding high social position or knowing any social prestige. You can be powerful without possessing a single implement that gives modern men and modern nations a sense of power. You can be happy with a happiness that is true joy of heart and gladness of soul without any of the tinseled pleasures of the senses. You can be safe with a security unobtainable by any material means if you will but listen to Me and learn wisdom. I, your God, am wishing you, am willing you a Merry Christmas. I am showing you the way to that merriment."

St. Bernard's conclusion after hearing such words from the Word is sharp: "Either Jesus Christ is deceived, or the world is in error." You know the only alternative in that disjunction which you can take. So God is telling you that the secret of happiness and the source of true joy lies in *being*, not in having. You can *be* rich without having any riches; *be* wealthy without possessing any wealth; *be* great and powerful without holding any power or greatness; you can *be* happy and even filled with joy without having anything to pamper the body, give pleasure to the senses, or comfort to the earthly frame. The luxuries of life are not necessary for the loftier life. To be all that God made you to be, you need only what this Babe has come to give: *grace!*

Now you are at the heart of the Christmas mystery and the miracle of love. *Puer natus est nobis; Filius datus est nobis* —"A Child is born to us; A Son is given to us." There is the central core of this feast and its fact. God is given to us in the guise of a Babe just born. But God's Gift must be accepted before the rapture God wants you to know can ever be felt. The Fathers and Doctors of the Church have echoed and re-echoed the truth John the Beloved put in his Prologue. Augustine said: "The Son of God was made man that men might become the children of God." St. Bernard asks: "Why

L
G-O-D
V
E

56

did God become man except that we men might become like God?" Yet, what are those but paraphrases of what St. Paul said to the Galatians: "God sent his Son, born of a woman, born under the Law, that he might redeem them that were under the Law, that we might receive the adoption of sons" (4:1–7). And what is that but an interpretation of John's immortal, almost unbelievable words, the words that tell you what Christmas is and why it makes you merry? "As many as received him," says St. John, "he gave the power of becoming sons of God; to those who believe in his name: who were born not of blood, nor of the will of the flesh, nor of the will of man, but of God" (Prologue).

Listen to the divine Infant saying "I was born of woman that you might be born of God."

The depths to which God descended that first Christmas night when He, infinite Glory, Majesty, and Might, was found as a helpless Babe in a trough from which animals fed, is the measure of the heights to which He would lift you. He was born far below Himself that you might be reborn limitless leagues above yourself. But His lowliness is the only way to His heights; His humility, obscurity, simplicity, and poverty the only way to His riches, grandeur, and glory; His scorn for luxury and comfort the only way to happiness and joy.

St. Paul had said "The sensual man perceiveth not the things that are of God" (1 Cor. 2:14). St. Bernard in commentary on those words exclaimed: "Now he may; for the Word is made flesh. If the sensual man can comprehend only what concerns the flesh, let him hear the Word even in the Flesh! This Birth of Christ calls out, so to say, in a manner intelligible even to the carnal minded" (Third Sermon for Christmas Day).

No one, then, need miss the message of God. Actions speak louder than words even for the Father. That is why He *gave* His Son. The same holds true for the Son. That is why He *became* Flesh.

L
G-O-D
V
E

57

"I am come that they may have life; and have it more abundantly.". . . "God so loved the world, as to give His only begotten Son; that whosoever believeth in Him, may not perish, but may have life everlasting." That is what you want. And God is here to tell you how to acquire it.

God is revealing to you a sense of values. He is telling you what is of real worth. This "holy Infant so tender and mild" as the carol has it, speaks stern, strong language from His lowly crib. His tiny hands, too feeble to grasp your little finger firmly, fling aside, with giant gesture, those cumbersome things worldlings so crave. But the lesson of all lessons is in the light of His eyes. Read there your own worth. It is *infinite*. Because of you God became a baby. The price God the Father paid for you is in the crib. The price God the Son will pay for you is seen in the human life God has assumed that He may lay it down so that you may live forever! Christmas tells you your worth. But it is read better in the name that was given the Christ eight days after His Birth.

WHAT'S IN A NAME?

Ponder well the name of *Jesus*. That, in all reality, is the word God uses to greet you; for it means Saviour, and in that lies the full meaning of Christmas; for it is the glad tidings, the great joy that God gives to all mankind.

Gabriel had said to Mary: "Behold: you are to be a mother, and to bear a son, and to call him *Jesus!*" That was the first name that Gabriel gave; for it was the name God the Father wanted the world to hear. The other titles of "Son of the Most High," "Holy," and "Son of God" came after this name which means so much to man.

Mary replied to Elizabeth's greeting with her *Magnificat*, and in its first verse she tells that her joy lies "in God her Saviour" — her Jesus!

L
G-O-D
V
E

Zachary has his tongue loosed at last and breaks out into his glorious *Benedictus*, blessing God for visiting his people and bringing about its redemption — its Jesus!

58

The Child is born and an angel surrounded by the glory of God appears to shepherds and says: "Listen: I am bringing you good news of great joy which is in store for the whole nation. A Savior — a *Jesus* — who is the Lord Messias, was born to you today in David's town."

Listen to God speaking through the liturgy. The Midnight Mass has an Epistle which says: ". . . the grace of God our Savior — our Jesus — both appeared." The Mass of Aurora gives you one that reads: "the goodness and kindness of God our Saviour — our *Jesus* — hath appeared"; a Communion prayer that says: "Rejoice, O daughter of Sion; shout for joy, O daughter of Jerusalem: behold! thy King will come to thee, the Holy One, and the Saviour — the *Jesus* — of the world." Then in grand crescendo the Third Mass of the Day tells you in Gradual, Gospel, Secret, Communion, and Postcommunion that Jesus is here and that "the whole earth hath seen the salvation — the *Jesus* — of Our God."

But it is in the Mass of New Year's Day that God speaks most clearly and shows you what Christmas is. In the Psalm verse of the Introit He commands you to sing a new canticle — a new Christmas carol — "Sing to the Lord," He says, "a new canticle: for He hath done wonderful things." The Collect tells you what those wonderful things are when it has you pray: "O God, who by the fruitful Virginity of the Blessed Mary hast given to mankind the rewards of eternal salvation. . . ." St. Paul follows immediately with that Epistle to Titus, wherein he says "the grace of God our *Saviour* hath appeared to all men." But it is the Gradual that tells the truth most fully: "All the ends of the earth have seen the *salvation* of our God"; then commands all the earth to sing joyfully to the Lord. That is not enough. It goes on to specify and sing: "The Lord hath made known His *salvation:* He hath revealed His Justice in the sight of the Gentiles." That word Justice really stands for Jesus, as the Alleluia verse of the same Gradual tells you. "God, who at sundry times and

L

G-O-D

V

E

in divers manners spoke in time past to our fathers by the
Prophets, last of all in these days, hath spoken to us by
His Son."

Then comes the Gospel. The shortest Gospel of all the
year opens the civil year for you. It contains but one sentence; yet in that sentence you have the name above all
names; the word with which God greets and gifts you; the
name which explains God's purpose in becoming man; the
name, the only name men need to know in order to look up
with joy, and head through life's valleys and over life's hills
with faces alight with confidence and hearts athrob with a
sense of their own infinite worth. The Gospel reads:

> And after eight days were accomplished, that the Child should be
> circumcised, his name was called Jesus, which was called by the
> angel, before he was conceived in the womb (Lk. 2:21).

You must have noted the similarity between this Mass
and the Third Mass of Christmas Day. It is only proper; for
New Year's Day is the Octave of Christmas. The one feast
of the birth of our Lord and Saviour is celebrated liturgically
for forty days and ends fittingly on the Feast of the Presentation and Purification; for it is on that day that God is offered
to God — and that is the essence of the Mass. So you see
how nicely articulated are the various feasts in this Christmas
cycle. A Child is born — He is God. Then that Child is named.
He is called Saviour. Finally He is presented in the Temple;
for it is only by offering Himself to God — and being accepted
by Him — that men will be saved, and this Child live up
to His name of *Jesus*.

Twice before His birth an angel came to earth to tell
those holy two who would be known as His earthly parents
that the Child's name was to be Jesus. Gabriel announced it
first to Mary that day of days when Creation's *Fiat* was
echoed by a *Fiat* that brought Re-creation. Then some months
later when that just man, Joseph, was thinking of what to do

L
G-O-D
V
E

60

about Mary, an angel, whom many believe to have been the same Gabriel, came to the perplexed carpenter and said: "Joseph, son of David, fear not to take unto thee Mary thy wife, for that which is conceived in her, is of the Holy Ghost. And she shall bring forth a son: and thou shalt call his name Jesus. For he shall save his people from their sins" (Mt. 1:20–22). You see why many think that message came from the lips of Gabriel. It is of a piece with what he told Zachary, Mary, and the shepherds (if it was Gabriel who spoke to the watchers of the flocks). But note how the angel interprets the name for the two. To Mary he announced that "He shall be great, and shall be called the Son of the Most High; and the Lord God shall give unto him the throne of David his Father; and he shall reign in the house of Jacob forever. And of his kingdom there shall be no end" (Lk. 1:32, 33). Such an interpretation supposes intimate knowledge of the Old Law Prophets and all they had announced about the Messias and His kingship. The names of Juda and David ring through them like a refrain. Mary knew then that her Son was to be Saviour. But to Joseph the clear, unmistakable interpretation is given when the angel says: ". . . for he shall *save* his people from their sins." Christ's mission is contained in His name. And there you have the fusion of these feasts — Christmas and New Year's — into one. It was not enough for the Babe to be the Christ — the anointed of God; He had to become, as it were, Jesus — the saviour of men. In the Nativity and the Name Day conjoined you have your compound word Christmas, which gives you the essence of the "good news" and of the "great joy" that good news brings: you have been *saved* for God by God.

The announcement that he will free us from sin — tremendous though it be — is only the negative aspect of God's word. To be delivered from your sins and the consequences of them is a gift of measureless magnitude; yet it is the smaller portion. His Christmas gift to you is birth, life, divinity! THE POSITIVE SIDE

61

You have already heard Augustine, Bernard, St. Paul saying that God became man that men might become like God. You have heard Jesus Himself say: "I was born of woman that you might be born of God." You have listened to St. John saying: ". . . to as many as received him, he gave them power to be made the sons of God, to them that believe in his name, who are born, not of blood, nor of the will of the flesh, nor of the will of man, but of God." There is the positive side of the feast and the fact. There is the real reason for the world-wide joy on this day of Christ's birth. It marks the beginning of a new race of men — those who would be "born of God"; those who would share the divine life with God by becoming partakers of His nature through the grace which the *Christ* would win by living up to His name of Jesus and saying *Mass!*

In very truth you celebrate your own birthday when you commemorate the birthday of Christ; for you believe in His name and you are born of God!

With what more telling truth, with what more forceful fact could one begin the New Year than the one Holy Mother Church, and thus God Himself, gives you? The year, and every day in the year, is dedicated to Him who was named Jesus — a name of such awe that "every knee on earth, in heaven and in hell bows in adoration" at its very pronouncement, and yet of such sweetness that ages on ages have sung *Jesu, dulcis memoria* — the very remembrance of that name is sweetness itself — *dans vera cordi gaudia* — giving to the heart a joy that is true joy. In a sermon which alone would have won for him the title of "Mellifluous" St. Bernard says "The Name of Jesus is Light, and Food, and Medicine. Light when it is preached; Food when meditated; Medicine when invoked. . . . Whence came there into the whole world so bright and sudden a light except from the preaching of the Name of Jesus? . . . Nor is it Light only; it is also Food. . . . For what is there that so feeds the mind

L
G-O-D
V
E

62

that meditates upon this Name? What is there that so restores
the wearied faculties, strengthens virtue, gives vigor to good
and holy habits, and fosters chastity? Every food of the soul
is dry if not steeped in this unction; insipid, if not seasoned
with this salt. If you write, I relish not your writing unless
I read there the name of Jesus. If you teach or converse
with me, I relish not your words unless I hear you say the
name of Jesus. Jesus is honey to the mouth, music to the
ear, gladness to the heart. More, it is Medicine. Is any among
you sad? Let Jesus come into his heart and his mouth echo
His Name, saying *Jesus*, and lo! the light of the Name dis-
perses every cloud and brings sunshine back again. . . . Let
us see how all this comes to pass. . . . When I pronounce this
name of Jesus, I bring before my mind the Man, who by
excellence is meek and humble of heart, sober, chaste, merci-
ful, and filled with everything that is good and holy, nay,
who is very God Almighty — whose example heals me, and
whose assistance strengthens me. I say all this when I say
Jesus. Here I have my model: for He is a Man; here I have
my help: for He is God" (XV Sermon on the Canticle).

There you have your greeting and your gift and your goal!
In the name Jesus you clasp the cave, the crib, and the Bread
of Life that is cradled there. For you see how this holy night
of His birth looks forward to that other holy night before
His death when He became Jesus in fact as well as name.
He is lying in a manger — a manger is something shaped so as
to hold food. You see His body of flesh which He has taken
from Mary's immaculate flesh. One Thursday night He will
take bread, bless, break and give to His disciples saying:
"Take ye and eat; This is My Body." You see His blood now
pulsing at His baby temples, flushing His delicate flesh. One
Thursday night He will take wine, bless, give to His disciples
saying: "Drink ye all of this; This is My Blood." The body
of this Child will yet be given for you. That blood will yet
be poured out — all of it — for you! Then He will be Jesus;

L
G-O-D
V
E

63

and you will be saved; for Christ will have made Christ-Mass.

And God says all this to you in the Mass at Christmas. "While all things were in quiet silence and the night was in the midst of her course. . . ." Thus begins one of the Masses within the Octave, reminding you of the *Paschal Lamb,* which saved the People of God when the angel of the Lord, in the middle of the night, went through the land of Egypt slaying every first-born.

LOVE AND
JUSTICE

That brings you to the virtue most revealed by this fourth letter in the word God is using to greet you. It is the cardinal virtue of Justice. It is not often that you think of justice in connection with love, but in God the two are one. His justice is but another manifestation of His love. And never is that more clearly seen than in the One who was born on Christmas Day and named Jesus on New Year's.

The first man had offered insult to an infinite God. Since offense is measured by the One offended, you can see how this was an infinite offense. But while Adam could give infinite offense he could not make infinite reparation nor offer adequate apology to Infinity. For reparation is measured by the dignity of the one repairing. Justice would never be satisfied had not God, the Infinite, become Man . . . become Christ Jesus. So that the Man in Him could suffer for the man who had sinned; and the God in Him make the suffering of infinite worth, so that the God who had been sinned against would be satisfied. The apology for the insult of sin had to be a Theandric apology; it had to come from a God-Man. It came from Christ Jesus — and Justice received its due. But when one says Christ Jesus, as Paul so often did, one is really saying Christ-Mass or Christmas.

L
G-O-D
V
E

In the Masses of Christmas Day and New Year's you will find this notion of Justice heavily stressed. The Epistle of St. Paul to Titus, so often used in these Masses, holds a command that you be just to God, just to your neighbor, just to yourself. You are obligated to that if you "believe in His name" and are "born of God"; for you cannot call upon the name of Jesus, nor call yourself a Christian unless you live as Paul says: *sobrie, juste et pie* — that is, you will have a Merry Christmas and a Happy New Year only if you fulfill your duties toward yourself by living *soberly,* your duties toward your neighbor by living *justly,* your duties toward God by living *piously.* In other words, you must live a life of love; for Christian justice *is* love.

To do any of these things you must accept the gift God gives you in His greeting. You must hug God to your heart — *literally!*

In Dresden before night fell over Germany, there hung that masterpiece by Corregio, which is named "Holy Night." In it you see Mary bending over the Child who was born this Holy Night. The marvelous part of this painting is the splendor of the light that suffuses the Maiden-Mother's face and whole body. Its soft golden brilliancy suggests that Mary had embraced the sun and its molten gold had clung to her. The beauty of that picture is founded on deepest truth: *the effect of nearness to Christ.* He, the fountainhead of all grace, had made her full of grace. He, the Light of the World, had reflected His golden splendor upon her — the very Mirror of Justice.

Now that picture will give you some idea of what God means when He greets you at Christmas. He wants you to hug the Child, and come away from the embrace carrying Christness with you.

But again the warning must be given. To hug this Child *is* delight; but it is a contact that carries obligations with it. His tender flesh on prickly straw says exactly what Paul says: Live *soberly;* that is, deny your lower self in order to be true to your better self. Be just even to yourself! The fact that He is Jesus says: Live *justly.* Give your neighbor what is his due; that is, be ready to lay down your very life for him. That may seem more than justice demands, but you are to

L

G-O-D

V

E

remember that Jesus, in giving Himself to you, gives you the power to live as He lived. And He died in order to live justly to His neighbors — you and all the rest of us who are sinners. Christian justice is love — and love knows no measure. Truly, Love does such things.

Surely you hear Jesus saying: Live *piously;* that is, give God His due. Which means give Him your entire self by doing just what He has commanded. To live piously and give God His due does not mean running off to devotions and rattling off numberless prayers by rote. It means being *devoted.* That, in its turn, means doing God's will in your particular state of life — even if that will calls for a cave, a crib, swaddling bands, and beasts! Learn from this coming of Christ into the world that every single event in your life is a "coming of Christ" into your world. In other words, be conscious of the will of God in every happening of day and night. Be able to say with Jesus "in the head of the Book it is written of me: I come to do thy will, O God!" (Ps. 39:8.) As life goes on, be able to echo the same divine Son by saying: "I do always the things that please Him." Then as life ends, you will be able to repeat those glorious words of the Word: *Consummatum est!* — I have *done* thy Will, O God." That is living piously, religiously, godly; for it is living as Christ Jesus lived — a life of love. That, precisely, is what devotedness means, and what justice is!

A NEW
YEAR'S
RESOLUTION

L
G-O-D
V
E

So God's greeting makes it incumbent on you to take one New Year's resolution: to *live up to the Holy Name of Jesus.* That is your goal. That is the glory set before you by God's greeting and His gift. God means that you are to *be* Jesus — be a Saviour! That is the dignity conferred on you. Nothing less. But that dignity is also a destiny and a duty. *Noblesse oblige!* You, by believing in His name and being born of God, are obligated to *be* Christ Jesus. So you see how your New Year's resolution really means that you are determined to be true to yourself — *in Christ Jesus.* For the new race of men who were born this night and received this name belong to God just as truly as did the body and blood Jesus took from Mary, His mother. You become His member! The Head was born that first Christmas night and laid in a manger. But just as truly as He assumed that nature when Mary said *Fiat,* so truly did He assume your individual nature into His body when you were baptized.

The holy name of this newborn Babe should beat in your blood and live in the very marrow of your bones and being; for you were baptized, that is, reborn, in that name; you were nourished, that is, given your heavenly Food, in that name; chrism was put on you to mark you as soldier and knight, in that name; and when you tarnished your honor, soiled your soul by sin, it was in that name that you were cleansed, and, as it were, born anew. Every prayer the Church has offered for you, every sacrament she has given to you, every act she has performed for you, has been in that name. And when the hour is come when you are to go forth to your eternal home and your life with God face to face, she will bid you "Go forth!" in His name. Then after celebrating Christ-Mass over your body and for your soul, she will pray God to give you eternal rest in His name. For "there is no other name in which you can be saved" (Acts 4:12). Since justice is charity, and charity begins at home, you must save your own soul if you would be just to God. Hence your incessant prayer is "Jesus, *be* Jesus to me!" To implement that prayer you will follow St. Paul's injunction: "Whatever you say or do, let it always be in the Name of the Lord Jesus" (Col. 3:17).

Jesus Himself was very conscious of His name and its value. That is why He has John the Beloved report among His final words: "If you ask the Father anything in my Name, he will give it you" (Jn. 16:23).

You have seen the one Word God uses; let us continue our spelling.

L
G-O-D
V
E

THE PRESENTATION IN THE TEMPLE
BY PHILIPPE DE CHAMPAIGNE
ROYAL ART MUSEUM, BRUSSELS, BELGIUM

S -A-V-I-O-

Offerings Speak More Loudly
Than Even God's Word

O, in the word God uses as greeting, stands for *offerings*. It tells of that hour when Mary stood radiant with joy, as she presented the Child in the Temple. She was as much a priestess as the New Law will ever know; for her immaculate hands were very like a paten of shining white gold as there rested on them the Living Host. Surely the deafest of mortals can hear the immortal God accenting the second syllable of the word Christmas as Mary makes Presentation to God of this her Son who is also the only-begotten Son of the Father. As she stands there before the priest of the Old Law, fulfilling the command God gave through Moses, what Catholic does not hear every priest of the New Law fulfilling the command given by Christ the night before he became Jesus in fact? Mary's gift to God of God's gift to us could only be made meaningful by those prayers said now by every ordained Christ who holds wheat and wine in outstretched hands and says: *Suscipe, Sancte Pater, hanc immaculatam hostiam* — "Take and receive, O God, this all-immaculate Host"; and *Offerimus Tibi, Domine, calicem salutaris* . . . "We offer Thee, O God, this saving chalice."

Symbol most certainly of the Offertory of the Mass Christ Himself would say, is this Presentation of the Child in the Temple. Since Christ, without the Mass, would mean very

THAT SECOND SYLLABLE

69

little to you children of First Parents who offended the infinite God, this Fourth Joyful Mystery of Mary's Rosary, should always enable you to hear God greeting you. Jesus is but an Infant of forty days, yet in Him is housed all the Wisdom, Understanding, and Knowledge of the ages, and of eternity. He is Man — every inch of Him! But He is also God — with every attribute of Divinity. That is why He has two names: Christ — the anointed of God — and Jesus — the Savior of men. That is why Christmas is a compound word: Christ-Mass!

Forgive what may seem like the belaboring of a point, but the second syllable of the word Christmas is really the important syllable for you. Your eternal happiness was won not by Christ's birth but by Jesus' death! Heaven was opened to you not by what happened at Bethlehem but by what took place on Golgotha. Everlasting life with God was made possible for you not by Mary laying Jesus in the crib but by Christ laying Himself on the cross. That is why the Presentation in the Temple has such deep meaning for you. God is speaking again by symbols and signs, but to you of the twentieth century His voice is clear in the symbolized and the signified. Joseph purchased Mary's Child back from the service of God — to which the first-born male was obligated — by paying five shekels to the high priest. But you were bought back from the service of the Devil — to which all mankind, sprung from our First Parents, was destined — by thirty pieces of silver some high priests paid out that Mary's Son might be captured and given opportunity to say His First Mass. Christmas for you looks not only to the cave outside the lowest and least of Juda's cities, but more especially to the cross outside Juda's largest and holiest of cities. Moreover, when God greets you at Christmas He is speaking not only of the birth of His only Son, but of His life, death, Resurrection, and Ascension — all of which come to mind when we enter fully into the Mass.

L
G-O-D
V
E

70

Mary offers her only Child — her all! Joseph offers two turtle doves and five measly shekels — practically his all! Everything about this Presentation speaks of poverty, of lowliness, and all the suffering and hardships connected with both. And God is speaking to you through that poverty and lowliness and all that they connote. If you hear Him you will have what He wills you to have — a blessedly merry Christmas this day of feast and every day of your life; for you will have heard how every work of God is a *perfect* work! We have already learned that the crowded Inn and the closed doors of Bethlehem showed no lack of preparedness on God's part or imperfection in His plan or planning. The bare cave, the cold crib, the loneliness of the night were not blotches on the magnificence of that masterpiece we call the birth of Christ. God's works are perfect works. They ask for no sympathy; it is docility that they demand. The Presentation, this first note in the symphony of the Mass, teaches as eloquently as did the Silent and Holy Night of the Nativity. The lessons are the same; for God knows that we are dull pupils and that we will never have the Merry Christmas He wills us to have until we have learned proper values and the perfection in the things our blundering leads us to call imperfect.

Simplicity was called to the crib in the persons of the shepherds, but now as holy old Simeon totters forth to take infinite Wisdom in his arms and the wise old widow, Anna, comes from the shadows of the porches and the pillars we learn that no age, no acumen or lack of endowment, no stratum of society can ever have a monopoly on God. And when shortly we see the Magi in the presence of the Mother and Child we will learn that not even poverty, actual or spiritual, can have exclusive claim on Him who is the wealth of all the world. God is speaking to us and saying that there is no evil, no imperfection, no lack of artistic excellence in any of His works no matter how they may appear to our shortsightedness. He is saying that in all the universe there is only one blot, one

71

offensive sight, one disgusting fact — and that is sin. Poverty is no disgrace — else Jesus, Mary, and Joseph would not now be standing among the poor. Blindness, deafness, palsy — even possession by the devil, yes, and death itself can all be, and are meant to be, perfections in God's all-over plan. When Christ lived, such things were the occasions of miracles. And Christ lives today just as really as He lived two thousand years ago — and lives in our midst, with hands just as generous and heart just as powerful.

Was the man born blind a blot or a special brilliancy in the life of Christ? The praises of God that rent the air after Jesus had given him his sight answer for you. And what of the men sick of the palsy -- were they evidence that God had blundered in His making of men? What of the pitiful lepers — do they tell of a lack of power and perfection in the Omnipotent and All-perfect God? Not when you see the first rise, take up their beds and walk, and the second run off to show their fully cleansed skin to the priests. God is a sculptor in whose hand no chisel ever slips. God is a painter whose brush never leaves a smudge. God is the artist whose every work is a masterpiece.

You say your baby was born without a functioning brain. God says he could be baptized, he could be presented in the Temple, he could be made a member of Bethlehem's Babe. He could spend eternity with Gabriel and the whole angelic host singing: *Gloria in excelsis Deo*. Why not thank God, then, for the wondrous gift of an immortal soul despite the physically defective body in which He sent it?

A man has eyes that do not see and ears that do not hear. Surely here is an unfinished symphony. But can he not hear the voice of God sounding in his soul? Will he not see the face of God for all eternity if he returns God's Christmas greeting with a life of love? If he sees and hears God, what other music could he desire? What other symphony could be more complete?

L
G-O-D
V
E

72

Pause and realize all that these Mysteries are saying to you. For to truth-loving realists nothing is more irritating than baseless optimism. People who hear God speaking must be very, very strong. This Feast of the Presentation, which is really the climax of Christmas and the liturgical ending of Christmastide, has been giving you reason after reason for being ever optimistic and smiling in the face of a world whose countenance is all scowl. The reasons all reduce themselves to the one reason — the host and chalice Mary holds in the paten of her hands. Catholics are the realists of the Realists. They are men and women who never turn their face from actualities nor look at what the world calls physical evils only in profile. We demand front face and full view because we know with the certainty of faith that in all the wide world there is no imperfect work of God and that there is only one real evil — sin. Our proof of the perfection in all that exists can be drawn from the feast which begins in a dark cave outside Bethlehem and is climaxed near the Holy of Holies in Jerusalem's Temple; for the first spells *Christ* for us, while the second makes that word *Christmas*. And that compound word tells how the tumblers in the locks of heaven were set falling into place; how the angel at Eden's gates was set sheathing his fiery sword; how Paradise Lost became Paradise Regained — for us!

Mary's outstretched hands at the Presentation really fashion within us a citadel which, no matter how often it may be stormed, can never be taken. It stands in the deepest depth of our souls and is the citadel of faith. It is a sacred place where we are truly ourselves and where we meet God and His grace. It is a stronghold wherein we are ever at peace no matter what wars are being fought in the world. It is a center that knows perfect calm no matter what storms rage outside. It is the silent spot whence we hear God's Christmas greeting! And that is the source of our courage and our optimism.

L
G-O-D
V
E

CATHOLIC
REALISM

Catholics can point out realistically that there is cancer, polio, tuberculosis, leprosy; that our world is one huge hospital and our earth one immense graveyard. They will point to men and women minus valuable limbs; to the neurotic, the insane. They will even say "Naturally speaking these people are to be pitied." But because Mary presented Jesus in the Temple — and that Presentation was but symbol of the Offering He Himself would make of Himself outside the Temple and the City — they are quick to add: "But we Catholics never speak 'naturally.' Hence, these people if they co-operate generously are to be envied. They have a more important part in Christ's Mass and in Christmas than we who think ourselves able-bodied, full-souled, and sound of mind."

This lesson which shows God's loveliness in everything on earth — especially in those who might be looked upon as unfortunate; this mystery of poverty and purity gives us a conviction which nothing can shake as it implicitly says: "God lives, God rules, God loves each of us."

The Christ in Mary's hands is but forty days old. Yet it is by offering Himself to God that He conquered the strength of sin and death and shattered the bolts which barred heaven to all men. That is why every Christian, no matter what his physical condition, can rejoice. For he, too, can be offered to God in Christ Jesus!

This is a feast which sets aglow within us not only a faith in God, but a faith in our predestination. And these two faiths let us know that life is worth living and death worth dying.

St. Pius X, in a great encyclical* said that when Mary conceived Christ and carried Him in her womb, she was actually, though not physically carrying each of us who were predestined to be baptized into Christ. Since that is true, do you not see that when Mary held Jesus out in the paten

L
G-O-D
V
E

* *Ad diem illum.*

74

of her hands, she was holding out *you?* That is why Christmas is merry and meant to be so by God! For when Christ was born, a new race of men was brought into being; men who were to be *coadjutores Dei* — men who would help God! The splendor of that calling lies in the fact that no matter what our liabilities in the mental, physical, social, political, or economic line, we can be perfect workmen who turn out a flawless bit of work!

Mary, by this Presentation, has brought us deep into the heart of the Christmas mystery and faces us not only with the generosity of God but with the demand on our own generosity.

By holding the Maker of the world out to God she shows us that the one work of the world is to give glory to God. She also shows us that the one work of Christ is to repair the work of God. You see, do you not, that those two works are one? Well, in His Christmas greeting to you God is telling you that your life's work is to help Jesus repair and to aid the world in glorifying God. It is a tremendous role God gives you. But once you have grasped your own significance in the plan of Omnipotence your heart will ever be joyful for you will realize that you fill out Christ; that you are the latest syllable in the Word of God! St. Paul put it in a single phrase: *Pleroma Christi.*

CHRISTIANS CAN NEVER FAIL

Once we believe that with all our mind and will and strength, all life is glory! For we will never consider anyone as really "handicapped" or "underprivileged"; never look on any single human as other than sacred. This conviction changes the whole world of men and women and children for us. But the biggest change is wrought within us; for this offering of God to God, and our part in Divinity's plan, tells us that no matter what happens to us in life, *we can never fail.*

L
G-O-D
V
E

To grasp this truth the more clearly, look at the other offering we see in Christmastide and hear what God has to say to us through it.

On the sixth of January you celebrate the Epiphany. In the Eastern Church this Feast of the Magi is really *the* Christmas Feast; and when you look into the liturgy even of our Western Church, you begin to understand why it is such an important feast; for the differences between our beloved birthday of Christ and this day of His manifestation are profound and replete with truths as personal as your pulse!

For centuries in the early Church this was the feast that commemorated the birth of our Lord. You can see how the differences between His birth and His manifestation would color your attitude toward the Infant. At Bethlehem He is all helplessness and lovableness. But when the Magi come we see Him as King of the Jews, and instead of hugging Him to our hearts as we are prone to do at Christmas, we join the Wise Men in their adoration of His Majesty and offer Him what gifts we have.

This story of the Magi reads almost like a fairy tale. But is that not true of the entire Gospel? Are not all God's works marvelous and more wonderful than any fairy tale? Just think a moment on the truths we have been reviewing from the birth of sin in the human race through the fall of Adam, down to the birth of the Saviour of that race, thanks to Mary's conception of Christ and bringing Him forth in a cave. The mysteries of our religion far outshine the grandest creations of mythology. In the mystery of the Epiphany the actors God employs give you something much more magical than anything in the Arabian Nights.

A star of marvelous magnitude and brilliance suddenly lights the heavens. Far in the East, days and months and even years distant from Jerusalem, a tiny group of men see it. They are learned, these astrologers, and really merit the title of sages. Every book worth reading they have conned. From both Zoroaster and the Book of Numbers they knew about "the Star that was to arise out of Jacob and the sceptre that was to spring up from Israel" (Num. 24:16). They shared the

L
G-O-D
V
E

76

hopes of the Jews. They dreamed their own dreams of the
Messias that was to come. And now they prove the truth of
the wise saying that "an undevout astronomer is mad," by
setting off at once. . . . But let us look again at the gospel
story. Who can check his imagination from conjuring up all
the color of the Orient as he reads:

> After Jesus was born in Bethlehem of Judea, in the days of King
> Herod, a commotion arose in Jerusalem when Magi from the
> East arrived and inquired: "Where is the newborn King of the
> Jews? It was his star we saw in the East, and we came to offer
> homage to him."
>
> The news threw King Herod into consternation, shared by
> all Jerusalem. Assembling the whole body of the high priests
> and Scribes — the nation's Council — he inquired of them where
> the Messias was to be born. "At Bethlehem in Judea," they
> said to him. . . .
>
> Then Herod secretly summoned the Magi and, after carefully
> ascertaining from them the time during which the star had
> been visible, he sent them to Bethlehem with this injunction:
> "Go and make careful inquiry about the child, and when you
> have found him, report to me. I, too, wish to go and do homage
> to him."
>
> So they obeyed the King and went their way; and, unexpectedly,
> the star they had seen in the East preceded them till it came
> and stopped over the place where the child was!
>
> At the sight of the star they were supremely happy. And so,
> entering the house and seeing the child with his mother Mary,
> they threw themselves down to do homage to him. Opening
> also their treasure chests, they presented Him with gifts: gold,
> frankincense, and myrrh. But advised in a dream not to return to
> Herod, they departed for their country by a different route
> (Mt. 2:1–12).*

How clearly God speaks! He hangs a star in the very
firmament as a Christmas greeting to men. Note the catho-
licity of God. The heavens are open to the gaze of all.
The Chosen People had had their centuries of special favor.

L
G-O-D
V
E

---

* Kleist-Lilly translation.

They were, at the same time, a grace to all the peoples with whom they came in contact; for they were a revelation of God to every pagan people and tribe. But now God would make special manifestation of Himself to the Gentiles and use them as a means of revelation to the Jews. He would use wise men from the East in much the same manner He had used Moses and Aaron, Isaias, and Ezechiel. These Magi would arouse all Jerusalem to the fact that their King had been born!

Do you sense the difference between this feast and fact and the fact and feast you commemorate on December the twenty-fifth? The Magi are asking to see a King; the shepherds were sent over to see a Babe! January sixth brings us face to face with the majesty of our King and the special mission of our Christ. Listen how the liturgy prays over the first:

> O God, who, by means of a star, didst this day manifest Thine Only-begotten Son to the Gentiles; grant that we, to whom Thou hast already made Thyself known by Faith, may come at last to the vision of the beauty of Thy Majesty. Through the same Christ, Our Lord, Amen. (Collect from Mass of Epiphany.)

As the Octave moves on we are made to realize more and more the priestly significance of Christ and the feast, and the surprisingly personal import and impact it contains for each of us. This solemnity has much to tell us of our life's work; for it speaks imperiously of the need we have of offering ourselves, consecrating our entire beings, and living in closest communion with Him who received this day gold, frankincense, and myrrh from men, whom medieval legend has named Gaspar, Melchior, and Balthasar.

In his commentary on the liturgy, which he calls *The Light of the World*, Benedict Bauer, O.S.B., claims that the prayer proper for this time runs:

> Protect us, O Lord, who have *consecrated* ourselves to Thy service, that we may be *concerned* with *divine things*, and live

L
G-O-D
V
E

78

united with Thee in body and soul. Amen. (Sunday within Octave of Epiphany. Emphasis added.)

Does not that remind you of Mary's action the day of Presentation? Do you not see that your offering is a consecration; and your consecration a craving for perpetual communion? You cannot miss the Mass in this Feast of the Epiphany if you will ponder the Secret of the Mass for the day. It clarifies the entire mystery and specifies your life's work. It is God speaking more clearly than ever before and telling you how easy it is to make a perfect success of life. The liturgy puts it thus:

> Graciously regard, we beseech Thee, O Lord, the gifts of Thy Church, in which gold, frankincense, and myrrh are no longer offered, but He whom these mystic offerings signified is immolated and received: Jesus Christ, Thy Son, Our Lord. Amen. (*Secret* of Mass of Epiphany.)

Have you always believed that the Epiphany was just for Jesus? That the Magi came with their gifts just to gladden His heart? Did you think that Christ was to receive this day and not give? The liturgy disturbs such thinking, does it not? And remember, the liturgy is very especially the voice of God in your regard. So think carefully on those words "immolated" and "received" in that prayer of the Mass; they mean much toward your philosophy and theology of life. They mean very much to your happiness in time as well as eternity. They mean everything, in final analysis, toward your hearing God's greeting, accepting His gift, living His Gospel, and attaining your goal. The Magi were not only for Christ; they were and are for every Christian. Their gifts were not alone for the Child; they were also for everyone who would be incorporated into the Child as His mystical members. The star itself was for you!

You are faced with the identical situation to that of the Magi. You have seen His star. You must set off with great faith and fortitude. You must seek your God confident that

L
G-O-D
V
E

79

you will find Him. The desert over which you walk may be trackless, devoid of oases, minus even so much as a mirage. Your star may even black out as did the star of the Magi. You may not be as fortunate as the Wise Men; you may not find a Herod who will summon the council of the nation who will tell you that He is born in Bethlehem of Juda. But you will find Him — for God is faithful and He loves you with an undying love. He wants you to do what Mary and the Magi did. He wants you to make offering. He wants you to do what Jesus did. He wants you to be the offered! In briefest brief, God wants you to say Mass. That is why He made you. That is why He made the Christ. That is why He is greeting you with a gift, giving you a Gospel which tells you your goal. And the Wise Men from the East tell you that you are one who need never fail. In your one life's work — and the only real work of your life — you cannot fail, if you live in Christ Jesus, if you make your life a Christ-Mass!

By baptism you were made Christ. That means you were stamped in your soul with the lineaments of the Conqueror Christ. Therefore — yes, it is an immediate illation — therefore, you are unconquerable so long as you live *per Ipsum, cum Ipso, et in Ipso*. That is the truth wrapped up in the Feast of Christmas and the chain of feasts that complete its cycle, especially those of the Epiphany and the Presentation. This Child in Mary's hands, this Child whom Wise Men adore, is not only a Victim but the Victor. Therefore, you, when in Him, are invincible. Because He came to conquer, and succeeded in His conquest of sin and death, you, so long as you live in Him, can never fail. And that is precisely what God is telling to you when He greets you at Christmas.

You remember the story of Thetis, the Grecian goddess, mother of Achilles, who held her child by the tendon near the heel, and dipped him into the River Styx. He came out of those waters invulnerable except in that one spot near the heel; for the waters never touched that spot. Then there was

L
G-O-D
V
E

80

Siegfried, the hero of the German epic Nibelungenlied. You may recall that he bathed in the blood of a slain dragon, and came forth from the bath invulnerable except in the one spot between the shoulder blades where an oak leaf had adhered and which the blood never touched. Those two tiny spots proved fatal. Achilles and Siegfried were conquered despite their almost perfect invulnerability.

When Holy Mother Church took you to the waters of baptism she held you by no tendon near the heel, nor did she simply dip you into those wondrous waters. No, as St. Paul so graphically describes baptism, she dropped you into those waters that you might drown therein, then rise from their depths a new man, completely invulnerable because incorporated in the impassible Christ. That is how Paul describes the Sacrament to the Romans — and he wrote his description under the inspiration of the very Spirit of Truth. You have no spiritual Achilles tendon. You cannot be pierced by an arrow even in the one spot near your heel. And, unlike Siegfried, you have been bathed not in the blood of a slain dragon, but in the Blood of the slain Lamb of God — and no oak leaf adhered to your back as you were covered by that Saving Blood. You have been sheathed, as it were, in the impenetrable armor of the utterly impassible Christ. Therefore, Discouragement — that Goliath who has slain his thousands — can hurl what shafts he will at you without once denting your shield so long as you live in the Child of Bethlehem whom Mary presented and the Magi adored.

MOTHER CHURCH BATHES YOU TO INVUL- NERABILITY

The young especially need to hear that; for the prospect before them may seem anything but bright. This truth, which is a truth from the lips of God will steel them against discouragement and strengthen their souls against anything like disheartenment. The old need to hear God saying this as comfort for the years that are fled and stimulus for the time that lies ahead. At Christmas God showed you your worth. At the Epiphany it is your work He manifests.

L G-O-D V E

81

The liturgy tells us that gold was given as something befitting a King; frankincense as that which becomes God; and myrrh foretells the burial of the Christ. God tells you that gold, in your regard, signifies *offering*. The King of kings is your Brother. *Noblesse oblige.* Give gold! God tells you frankincense must come from you as *consecration*. It is fitting; for you are a child of God — made so by your belief in the Babe of Bethlehem and your baptism. Burn your incense! God tells you in loving tones that myrrh belongs to you and your giving; for you are to be Christ — therefore, a victim and a victor! You are to live in closest *communion* with Jesus; you are to die in Him, and rise in Him, and reign with Him. You are to make the Mass your life — and your life a Mass.

You learned that teaching from the first page of your catechism when you answered the question: "Why did God make you?" Perhaps you have even become familiar with the phraseology of St. Ignatius. "Man was created for this end: that he praise, reverence, and serve the Lord, his God. . . ." Ignatius calls that the "Fundamental Principle." He could have called it the culminating climax as well. For the Vatican Council restated his Fundamental Principle when it solemnly declared that "Man was created to manifest God's glory." The catechism, Ignatius, and the Council, all are saying that man was created by God *to give*.

And what you are to give is exactly what Jesus gave — yourself! All that you have. All that you are. And, like the Christ, you are to give it to God.

Ah, but to give a gift to God is the definition of *sacrifice*. From the dawn of time that is what the word has meant — *sacrum — facere —* to make sacred by setting it aside for God. And that is what it will go on meaning forever. That is why you were born. That is why you live. That is why God greets and gifts you: that you may make of your life a sacred thing. And in that one work, which is very exactly the one only work of your life, you need never fail. How

L
G-O-D
V
E

THE EPIPHANY
AFTER A PAINTING BY HEINRICH HOFMAN
PRIVATE COLLECTION, HAMBURG, GERMANY

dare I tell you that despite the disappointments, the frustrations, the bankruptcies strewn up and down the land like driftwood after a shipwreck or storm, you need never fail in your life's one work? The answer lies in Mary's hands as she stretches them out to God. The answer is the gift God gives you as Christmas greeting. The answer lies in Christ Jesus. Because He was offered, consecrated, and accepted, you need never fail. The sword of Damocles which dangles over the head of every human, suspended by a thin and seemingly ever thinning thread, holds no threat for you so long as you live in Christ Jesus and offer all you have, all you do, all you are *per Ipsum, cum Ipso, et in Ipso.* For then, not only is your sacrifice acceptable to God, it will be lovingly accepted.

That last word is *the* important word. As the Magi unpack their treasure chests, think what the word "accepted" means to them — and thus learn what it means to you. Had not Mary and Joseph in the name of Jesus accepted the gold, frankincense, and myrrh, never could those things, which had been offered, been called gifts; for a thing is not a gift when it is offered, but only when it is accepted. Especially when we speak of a sacrificial gift. In the long Advent of at least four thousand years during which the Jews were waiting for Christmas Day, countless sacrifices were offered to God, but it was only occasionally that they became gifts; for it was only occasionally that God showed that He accepted their offering by sending fire from heaven to consume the offering. It was the divine acceptance that changed slaughter into Sacrifice — not the oblation of the people. Fire was the sign in the Old Law. Fire is still the sign in the New. And it was the fire which was the uncreated glory of God, shining out from the eyes of the Infant in Mary's hands, that made the Presentation so acceptable to God, just as it will be the uncreated glory of God falling upon the corpse of Christ Easter morning, coming back to that wounded body with His glorious soul and ushering in the Resurrection that will tell us that

GIFTS MUST BE ACCEPTED

L
G-O-D
V
E

83

Friday's slaughter was Sacrifice *par excellence*. That uncreated fire fell from heaven not to burn but to beautify; not to consume, but to render incorruptible; not to devour but to endow with the splendor of immortality, to set those wounds glowing with the glory of God and give us a *Victima Perennis* — "a Victim ever living to make intercession for us," as St. Paul says — and a Victim in whom you can be an acceptable victim.

This truth is based on the axiom of philosophers: *Actiones sunt suppositorum* — which means "actions belong to the person who performs them, not to the members by which they are performed." For instance, my fingers are doing this typing, but the action belongs to the person. Your eyes are reading these lines, but the reading is an action that belongs to you — for you are the responsible agent. Now apply that philosophical axiom theologically. By baptism you were made a member of Christ's Mystical Body. You know that it is the person who owns the body, not the other way about. So whenever you act "in Christ Jesus" — and there is no other sensible way to act — your action is not only yours, the member, but very specifically the action of the Person who owns the Body of which you are a member.

ACTIONS
BELONG
TO THE
PERSON

The action is yours! You are the responsible agent. And yet, as St. Thomas, St. Augustine, Cajetan, and the whole Thomistic school has taught, Christ takes those actions and makes them His own — He, the Second Person of the Blessed Trinity. The physical body He took from Mary belonged to a Person who is Infinite, because He is God. All the actions He performed in that Body were what are called Theandric actions — actions of a God-Man, actions that were human, because proceeding from a human nature, but divine also because performed by a divine Person. Hence they were of infinite worth. But Jesus Christ is "the same yesterday, today, and forever." Hence, when His mystical members act, as St. Augustine always insisted, *He* acts.

L
G-O-D
V
E

Are you beginning to understand what God's greeting

really means? Your most ordinary action can be sphered in infinity; your normal daily life can "fill out" Christ's Passion and death if you but place it in the Child Mary holds in her hands and in the Heart of Him whom Magi adore. You are a person who can never fail — so long as you live *in Christ Jesus.*

But do not misunderstand God's greeting. Although His gift to you is such that you need never fail, you must understand in what success really consists. You may fail externally. You may fail in the eyes of your family, your friends, your foes. In the eyes of all your fellow men you may fail; but in the eyes of Him who sees aright you need never fail, and His are the only eyes that can see whether you succeed or fail eternally. To Him it is the Mass that matters — and the Mass is Christ — God's gift to you.

The word *Christ-mass* looms ever larger. It is the only reality. For the Mass is the heart of this Christmas season — and Christ is the Mass.

If you have made the Morning Offering according to the formula of the Apostleship of Prayer and League of the Sacred Heart this day, you are at this moment on thousands of golden patens and mingled with the wine in thousands of golden chalices. You are a particle in every piece of bread that will be transubstantiated; you are a drop in every cup of wine that will be consecrated. Three hundred thousand times and more this day and every day, you are held up to God as Mary is holding Jesus up — aye, even more sacredly and more ceremoniously! Three hundred thousand times and more you are offered to God with the words: *Suscipe, Sancte Pater* . . . Three hundred thousand times and more human lips will say over you "This is My Body. . . ." but the voice that breaks on the ears of God will be the voice of the Word — the very Word which He is using to greet and gift you. How can you be other than merry when you realize that at every mystic mactation of the unslayable-slain Lamb of God, the stigmata

L
G-O-D
V
E

85

of His Passion blaze with a brilliance that blinds all heaven — and you are a tiny flame in that Wondrous Light! Think of it — not a moment in your day or night passes without you having been held up to God as the Magi are holding out gold, frankincense, and myrrh this moment of the Epiphany — and you are being accepted because you live in the accepted Christ!

How could you fail when your every effort "in Christ Jesus" is held up to God the Father by hands that hold the print of Calvary's nails, and the Voice that breaks on your behalf is the same Voice that once said *Fiat* in the Garden of Gethsemani and gave us a Corpse that was God, a lifeless Body that was and is the Source of all supernatural life? How can you fail when your slightest act is latent with the possibility of saving a world so long as it is offered in Mary's Child? The science of success for you lies in living in Christ Jesus — and the secret of that science is in focusing on effort and leaving the effects to God. It comes down to saying the words of Consecration over your every movement — and leaving the miracle of transubstantiation up to Him.

SOME
SUCCESSFUL
FAILURES

That is what every successful failure has done. Take Leon Bloy for an example. In the sixty-eight years of his life he wrote thirty books of great beauty; yet he endured the agony of seeing the truth he had clothed in such splendor almost ignored. Still Leon Bloy went on focusing on efforts and leaving the effects to God. And God saw to it that those effects spelled failure, as the world judges such things. Bloy knew not only poverty, but destitution; yet he went on focusing on efforts, declaring: "There is only one sorrow. . . ." Only one sorrow for a man who lived eight years on little more than bread and water; only one sorrow for this man who had to watch his wife shiver and grow thin; who saw his two daughters die because God denied his brilliant works material success. "There is only one sorrow," Bloy declared: *"not to be a saint."*

L
G-O-D
V
E

There is a man who made the Mass of Christ his life —

and his own life the Christ-Mass. In all sincerity this man once wrote: "I live with but a single thought, a single emotion, and that so intense that my memory, my will, and the very nerve-center of my mental faculties is consumed by it. That thought is the thought of God — the Absolute."

Bloy's story is indeed that of a successful failure. But there is a greater failure than Bloy's which makes for a greater success; and God could tell you the story on no better day than Christmas Day. It is that of failure in the eyes of ecclesiastical superiors, failure in the eyes of God's own special representatives, such as that of Alphonsus Liguori, founder of the Redemptorists, and Basil Moreau, founder of the Congregation of the Holy Cross. The former was expelled from his Congregation by the Pope, the latter practically disowned by the Congregation he had founded. But they were not expelled from the congregation of the saints; for they knew how to focus on efforts and leave the effects to God; they made their lives a Mass by making Christ's Mass their life. How many other founders became gold, frankincense, and myrrh in the same way! Therese Couderc of the Cenacle, Cornelia Connolly of the Religious of the Child Jesus, Mary Ward of the Institute of Mary, to name some women; Camillus de Lellis, Louis de Montfort, Don Bosco, Joseph Calasanctius and on to Father Hecker, founder of the Paulists, to name a few men who could stand with Gaspar, Melchior, and Balthasar with gifts for God in their hands.

God may well point to Cardinal Newman on this Feast of the Epiphany and in connection with the Presentation, and tell you that you will never fail in the eyes of your contemporaries the way Newman failed in the eyes of his. As an Anglican he was too Catholic for his Anglican brethren. As a Catholic he was too Anglican for his Catholic confreres. In every major undertaking for the Church and God after his conversion he was thwarted by his fellow Churchmen. Rome itself stepped in and interrogated the saintly convert.

L
G-O-D
V
E

To use his own words he underwent a "penance of slander and unpopularity," which lasted for thirty years. In his old age he once said: "I offered Rome my heart. She did not accept it." But God did! That *Cor ad Cor Loquitur* on Newman's coat-of-arms is eloquent. Newman focused on efforts. And thousands, perhaps millions, pray to him today.

The Magi gave gold and frankincense, it is true; but never forget they also offered myrrh. God, as He greets you, may point to the Little Flower even as He points to the last offering of the Wise Men. She is the classical example of our day as one who failed gloriously and succeeded beyond all expectations. Most people know that as she lay dying one of her own fellow Carmelites asked: "What can be written about her? What has she ever done?" You know the answer: Nothing but make herself gold, frankincense, and myrrh. Nothing but offer herself in Christ Jesus to be wheat and wine and make herself the Mass. Nothing but hold herself out in the paten of Mary's hands all the days of her existence, saying what you must ever say: "This is my body. This is my blood. Take it, O God, for it is yours."

But why mention the syllables when we have the Word as the example *par excellence* of the triumph of failure?

THE
FAILURE OF
THE WORLD

It is not often that preachers turn your thoughts toward the corpse of Calvary on Christmas morning. Yet there is truth in the saying, "Christ was born to die." Still, it is only a half-truth; for He was born to die *and rise again!* There, precisely is the Gospel God gives you as Christmas greeting. You not only cannot fail, if you live in Christ Jesus, but you cannot die forever! For since Jesus rose from the dead, every death of a Christian is a resurrection.

The failures in life really do not matter; it is the failure in death that counts. Thanks to Christ and His Mass, thanks to God in His greeting and His gift, you need never fail in life or at death. You can be utterly fearless in the moment all men fear; you can be glowingly joyous at the hour the

L
G-O-D
V
E

88

world calls saddest of all — the hour and moment of your final acceptance by God in Christ Jesus, the hour and moment men name death but which Christian men and women know as *birth!*

The liturgy insists that this gift of myrrh was given to indicate the burial of the Christ. But we would err grievously if we ever looked upon that burial as anything other than a steppingstone to the Resurrection.

When God gives you His word of greeting at Christmas you can now hear Him add: "For you a holy, happy Eternity has already begun. For you neither time nor time's end holds any fears. You can be Fortitude itself; for what St. Paul said of My Christ is to be said of all true Christians: 'Death shall no more have dominion over Him!' (Rom. 6:9.) And what your Jesus said in general is to be taken by you as particular: 'He that liveth and believeth in Me shall not die forever'" (Jn. 11:26).

With Father Abram Ryan, the poet-laureate of the Lost Cause, you can look Death in the eye and say:

I greet thee, Time's dread Victor, and my wasted lips do sing:
Dread Death, I am thy Victor. Strong Death, where is thy sting?

It has none for men and women who live in Christ Jesus and place themselves in Mary's hands as did the Babe of Bethlehem for this Presentation in the Temple. Death is weak compared to the strength in those who make of themselves gifts for God — gold, frankincense, and myrrh. Because these offerings were accepted, God's greeting really goes out to a race of Titans whom Christ set marching on a granite stairway that leads to the glory of God. For them every day is Christmas Day, filled with the merriment of God.

Unless you grasp the truths Christmas tells about death, your grasp on the truths it tells about life is a feeble thing. Because Leon Bloy had heard clearly God's Christmas greeting he could look up at the hour of his death, when asked

L
G-O-D
V
E

by friends "What are you experiencing at this last hour, Leon?" and reply: "A consuming curiosity!" Of course. For he wanted to *see* God. He had heard Simeon sing *Nunc dimittis* after holding the Christ in his hands. What could Bloy do after holding the same Christ so often in his heart but sing his *Nunc dimittis* with a happy heart and have it mean what Simeon meant, not: "Now thou dost dismiss . . ." but: "Come, Lord Jesus, and take Your child Home!" That is death for the Christian.

Mother Janet Stuart, the saintly Madame of the Sacred Heart, in her last agony was heard to exclaim: "Oh, how He longs for me!" That is the perfect interpretation of God's Christmas greeting to you, just as it is perfect summation of all that is contained in this feast and fact. God *does* long for *you*, otherwise He would never have become a Child, nor would that Child, grown to manhood, have become a Corpse, to rise on Easter morning, shining with the glory that is God. You will never know how much God loves you and longs for you until you see Him face to face. But it is wisdom itself to ponder now at Christmas on His longing and His love.

Once you hear God's greeting clearly you will not only understand, you will live the lesson St. Gregory the Great drew from the lines of St. Matthew concerning the Magi: "And having received an answer in their sleep that they should not return to Herod, they went back another way into their own country." On that sentence Gregory, the holy Pope and Doctor of the Church, makes this comment:

> The Wise Men teach us a great lesson in that they returned by another way into their own country. By thus doing as they had been warned, they make known to us what we, too, should do. Our country, to be sure, is Paradise. And since we know Jesus, we are forbidden to return thither along the same way by which we left it. For we departed from our own country by pride, disobedience, the love of visible things, by tasting the forbidden food; but we must return thither by the way of tears, obedience,

L
G-O-D
V
E

90

contempt of visible things, and by curbing the desires of the flesh. . . .

Let us expiate our sins by tears, and in the words of the Psalmist: let us come before His presence with thanksgiving.

What the saint is saying is: Be a successful failure. Return to your home by a different way — not the way of the world, but the way He took who overcame the world — by way of the Mass! There is the star that will lead you to God. It is the only one that moves, and can be called His Star.

Sister Madeleva, of St. Mary's College, Notre Dame, ended one of her Christmas poems with the words:

We are thy stars, Little King,
And we scatter the gold of ourselves at Thy feet.

After hearing God speak you know that the poet nun has expressed the same theological truth that St. Paul spoke to his Ephesians: "Once you were darkness, but now you are a light in the Lord. Walk then as Children of the light. The fruit of light consists in goodness, justice and truth" (Eph. 5:8–10).

To be a "light in the Lord" means to be clothed in grace; for as Father Pius Parsch once said "Persons who are in the state of grace are *like the stars.*" Jesus once said "So let your light shine before men that they may see your good works and glorify your Father who is in heaven" (Mt. 5:16).

Again we are back at the fundamental reason for creation and for the Re-creation we are commemorating at Christmastide: the *glory of God the Father.* To glorify God is not only our duty, it is our towering dignity. We, utterly unconsequential beings, can give *glory* to the infinite God! Small wonder we can have a merry Christmas!

But you must place yourself in the hands of Mary as Jesus did at the Presentation, and place yourself in actuality as the Magi once placed you in the symbols of gold, frankin-

A LIGHT IN
THE LORD

L
G-O-D
V
E

91

THE FLIGHT INTO EGYPT
AFTER A PAINTING BY HEINRICH HOFMAN
PRIVATE COLLECTION, DRESDEN, GERMANY

S~A~V~I~O~U~

With Earnestness and Urgency
God Gives You Your Goal

U is the next letter in the word. It stands for what at first shocks and greatly surprises those who know neither God nor themselves intimately. It stands for *urgency* — and while we mortals know much of urgency, especially as Christmas nears, we are astounded to have God, the ever tranquil, the utterly unhurried and eternally peaceful One, pressing us as He does with all that is connected with this letter in the life of His Word and the lives of all His Word's syllables.

Up to this point our world has been all brightness. The midnight sky of Christmas was lighted by stars; then the heavens opened and the glory of God shone forth. Nazareth was made brilliant by Gabriel and His message to Mary. Ain Karim was all gold and gladness; the name of Jesus is the name of the Light of the World; while the Offerings in the Temple, and in the humble home where the Mother and Child were found, colored our entire landscape and every horizon with beauty. But now God uses black. . . .

Master artist that He is, God introduces sudden contrast, to arrest us, alert us, shock us to sharpest attention.

We have seen that the Magi went back into their own country by a different route, and that the phrase "a different route" has a supremely practical application to our daily lives. We should be ever on the alert to catch pertinency to our

GOD'S
SUDDEN
CONTRAST

daily living in every phrase of Scripture. God now, in having St. Matthew go on with the story of Christ and giving us what is totally unexpected and completely mystifying, rouses our every emotion and keenly excites our curiosity. Matthew says:

> When they [the Wise Men] had departed, an angel of the Lord appeared, just in time, in a dream to Joseph, saying: "Rise! Take with you the child and his mother and flee into Egypt! Remain there till I give you further notice! Herod is on the point of searching for the child in order to take his life! (Mt. 2:13–15.)

That is the Kleist-Lilly translation. The translators have made every sentence of the angel a breathless exclamation. There is haste, excitement, urgency in every word.

What a message! This Child of whom the angel speaks is the One we heard angels, and Elizabeth, and Zachary, and Mary herself call Saviour; He is the One Joseph named Jesus when he circumcised Him; He is the one Simeon sang of as the Light to Gentiles and the Glory of Israel. Yet He is the one whom His parents must take by night and speed with Him into Egypt lest He be killed. What a strange Saviour is He who has to be saved! What a strange God who has to fly from His creatures! What a very strange King of kings who has to hurry into exile because of the threat of a petty king who is really His subject! What does God mean by this event so crowded with contradictions? Why this discord in the beautiful symphony we call Christmas? Why this change of color?

"All Scripture," says St. Paul, "is useful . . . for instructing in holiness, that the man of God may be perfect, fully equipped for every good deed" (2 Tim. 3:16, 17).*

This letter in the word God uses to greet you, is an important letter, not despite its strangeness but because of it. Love for you prompted God to use it. As you have spelled

L
G-O-D
V
E

* Kleist-Lilly translation.

out His word you have learned so much of that love that you might easily be lulled into false complacency. Shepherds taught you that God hovered over you as the best of shepherds would over an especially loved lamb. They told of Divine Providence and proved to you that it means more than the governance of the universe; it means a paternal and particular interest in you and every breath you breathe. Angels and their annunciations stressed the fact that God had not only made you great, but made you for great things — and these could be perfectly accomplished by a simple, sincere *Fiat*. The visit of the Virgin gave you, through the *Magnificat* and the *Benedictus*, along with Elizabeth's contribution to the "Hail Mary," not only the most beautiful Christmas carols that can be sung, but true insight into the might and the mercy of your God and His unalterable fidelity in your own personal, private regard. His Incarnation and the imposition of the name Jesus told you your worth as only God could tell you. Offerings told you your work, and the impossibility of failing in that work so long as you live in Him who is named Jesus. What can that add up to but a confidence that can easily become complacency?

God would never have that! He wants you to be merry at Christmastide, but at no time does He want you to be foolishly complacent. That is why He has His Son, that Son's Mother, and her chaste spouse know real hardship, experience all the fears that accompany flight from tyranny. Omnipotence, who by a mere act of His will, could have reduced Herod to less than the worms that were finally to consume him, becomes Impotence in the hands of a weak girl-mother. Omniscience, who knew all Herod's plans and the very gestures Herod's soldiers would make, becomes a Child who gives every appearance of complete helplessness as he nestles in Mary's frightened arms and allows the fearful Joseph to find his way across the dark desert. It was dark; for God the Holy Ghost tells us that Joseph "arose, and taking the Child, and His Mother

L
G-O-D
V
E

95

with Him, withdrew by night into Egypt." The only word in that translation that is weak is the word "withdrew." If Joseph was as prompt in obeying as that verb "arose" testifies and the phrase "by night" implies, then he and Jesus and Mary *fled* into Egypt; they stumbled out into the darkness, and hurried in fright down to the desert.

Up to now what have you heard but melody? The shepherds' song, the angels' song, the song of Mary and Zachary, the magnificent song of Simeon. But now into that music and sweet melody comes weeping and wailing and the death screams of baby boys. Matthew tells it briefly, yet fully.

> When at last Herod realized that he had been tricked by the Magi, he flew into a fierce rage and issued orders to massacre all the male children in Bethlehem and the whole vicinity who were two years old or under, reckoning by the time he had ascertained from the Magi. It was then that the prediction made through the prophet Jeremias was fulfilled:
>
> > "A cry was heard at Rama,
> > there was weeping and sore lament.
> > Rachel wept for her children;
> > she would not be consoled,
> > because they were no more." (Mt. 2:16–18.)*

To get correct ideas of what went on, let us do away with some false ones. First, remember that Bethlehem was a very small town — "too small to be among the chiliarchies of Juda." The few farms surrounding it, which were gathered together under that term "the whole vicinity," were neither numerous nor large. Modern critics, with the help of expert archaeologists, estimate two thousand to have been the number of inhabitants in the whole place at the time Herod flew into his rage. Then working on normal statistics concerning birth rate and number of boys usually born in two years to a specified number of parents, they arrive at the conclusion that the medieval commentators with their number of 144,000

L
G-O-D
V
E

---

* Kleist-Lilly translation.

slain were misled by the Epistle in the Mass for the Feast of the Holy Innocents. That Epistle is from the mysterious passage in the Apocalypse wherein the Seer of Patmos tells that he "heard a sound from heaven like the sound of many waters and like the sound of loud peals of thunder. The sound I heard was like that of harpists playing on their harps. They sang a new song before the throne and before the four living beings and the elders. No one could learn the song except those one hundred and forty-four thousand who had been purchased from the earth" (Apoc. 14:2–5).*

But the medieval scholars were not the only ones to err. Even today the Syrians number 64,000 as having been slain, while the Greek liturgy says 14,000. The numeral 4 in all those numbers may tell of a common source, and even of a common means of erring: copyists in monasteries often got sleepy!

Bethlehem was small; the vicinity around was even smaller; so Father Knabenbauer, who says that the number of Innocents slain was "twelve to fifteen, twenty at the most," and all modern commentators, who say twenty is the limit, more than likely are correct.

But why did God allow even twelve to be slain? Why break the hearts of a dozen Rachels? There must be an infinitely wise purpose and it must have to do with your Christmas happiness. Why does God inject this strident note into His Christmas carol?

St. Augustine calls it "a glorious martyrdom, though a cruel spectacle." That is the note that causes trouble. It is easy, WHAT and it is true, to exclaim as did Augustine: "O how happily WAS GOD'S born were they whom eternal life met on the threshold of PURPOSE? existence!" (First Sermon on the Innocents.) Like him, practically all subsequent rhetoricians have grasped the happy phrasing of Prudentius in his Epiphany Hymn, and spoken

---

*Kleist-Lilly translation.

of the "infant martyr flowers." Augustine, in his third sermon on the Innocents, states: "Rightly are they called 'flowers of the martyrs' whom, in the mid-winter of unbelief, a hoar frost as it were of persecution caused to bloom like the primal buds of the Church."

St. John Chrysostom would relieve us of the pain of sympathy by reminding us that the babes did not really suffer. In his fourth sermon on the Innocents he says: "Infancy, unconscious of suffering, bore away the palms and crowns of martyrdom. True martyrs of grace, they confess without voice; knowing not why, they actually fight; and though completely ignorant of it, they conquer; though unconscious of death, they die — thus do they bear away the palms and seize the crowns."

True, all gloriously true: the infants knew no great suffering; they were too young. They did not realize the battle they were in nor the victory they achieved until Ascension Day when He whom they had saved came to lead them to heaven. Fortunate indeed were the children who set Rachel weeping; but what of Rachel — who or what could comfort her?

Rachel, in Hebrew, means *sheep*. And who can fail to be moved as she laments the death of her lambs? They, because by their deaths saved the life of the very Lamb of God, rejoiced the nine choirs of heaven and the infinite heart of the Triune God. The Infants themselves knew unspeakable joy on this day of their slaughter; for as St. Augustine boldly states: "Behold, the profane enemy could never have benefited the little ones by kindness as much as he did by hatred. Do you ask how? Simply because he gave them the dignity and glory of Eternal Life almost before they had received the temporal one."

The little ones were real martyrs, never doubt it. And God stresses the idea of martyrdom in these earliest days of the Octave of Christmas. We monks have only ended the singing of Prime for this glorious Feast when we hear in the

L
G-O-D
V
E

98

Martyrology the chant of tomorrow's celebration: that of St. Stephen, the Prince of Martyrs. The following day we commemorate St. John, the soaring Eagle of Patmos, and read of his martyrdom on that Isle. But it is not until the Feast of the Holy Innocents that we have the circle completed, as St. Bernard so eloquently taught. He tells you what we have been endeavoring to have you hear as he probes into the urgency and earnestness of God. He does so by showing you the connection between the three feasts that immediately follow Christmas. They all have to do with your goal; for each teaches about *martyrdom*. "In St. Stephen," says the holy Abbot of Clairvaux, "we have both the act and the desire of Martyrdom; in St. John we have but the desire; in the Holy Innocents we have but the act." Knowing well that many will object to calling these babies of two years and under "martyrs," he faces the difficulty in this fashion: "Will anyone doubt that a crown was given these Innocents? . . . If you ask me what merit they could have that God should crown them, let me ask you what was the fault for which Herod slew them? What! Is the mercy of Jesus less than the cruelty of Herod? and will you have it that while Herod could put to death these Babes who had done him no injury, Jesus, for whom they died, may not crown them with life?

"Stephen is a martyr by a martyrdom of which men can judge . . . John was a martyr by a martyrdom only angels could see; but the Innocents were martyrs to no other eye than Thine, O God! Man could find no merit; angel could find no merit; but Thou didst manifest both the power and the excellency of Thy Grace in them. Thus, as the Psalmist had predicted: 'out of the mouths of infants and sucklings Thou hast perfected praise.'" (Sermon for Feast of Holy Innocents.)

That is the line Holy Mother Church uses to open the Mass on this heart-warming feast. She adds a phrase St. Bernard omitted but on which we must pause and ponder, GOD'S ENEMIES AND YOURS

99

for it points the lesson we are to learn from this letter. The *Introit* says: "Out of the mouths of infants and sucklings thou hast perfected praise, O God, *to confound thine enemies.*" God knows that He has three great enemies who will do all in their power to keep you from hearing His greeting, accepting His gift, living His Gospel, and attaining your goal. They are the World, your own Flesh, and the Devil. Because of these three enemies you have this Feast of the Holy Innocents and this Flight into Egypt. To make your Christmas merry, Rachel weeps and will not be comforted as Mary and Joseph hurry into Egypt. In short, to confound His and your enemies, Innocents must die.

We must resolve this discord slowly; study this consummate artistry with great care.

This world is God's world. Therefore, it is wondrous. Every atom in it came from His hands; and He saw that each was very good. It is no matter for wonder, then, if this world should attract you powerfully. Yet this creature of God is treacherous. Money, power, pleasure, fame, popularity, position in politics, economics, society are all creatures of God and all are very, very good; each can help you do what the Infants did — perfect His praise. But they are only means, not ends; they are only creatures, not the Creator; they are only instruments to help you praise Him who is to be praised by every instrument. They are only *toys*.

Christmas is the season for toys. They can teach you profound truths about yourself and your God, your life, and your goal. See what the mere sight of a toy does to children. Their every feature takes on new light and life; their hands go out to have and hold; their hearts are filled with pleasure. That is the proper function of toys — and God has filled the world with toys for you! Every creature can be looked upon as just that — a toy, given to you by God, for your pleasure. Indeed there *is* a Santa Claus. But His name is not Kriss Kringle nor even St. Nicholas. His name is that which the

L
G-O-D
V
E

100

Chosen People dared not pronounce, but which we of the New Dispensation love to say over and over again.

At what better moment than that of Christmas could we appreciate the differences our gift from God has brought to our world and to all of us who live after the birth of Christ? We are tempted sometimes to envy the Chosen People of God, with their passage through the Red Sea, their manna and quail and gushing water in the desert; their pillar of fire by night and their cloud by day; their Moses and Aaron and Josue. But we are wrong if we ever yield to that temptation; for we live in the fullness of time and have had the Law and the Prophets fulfilled before our eyes.

The Old Law was in many repects a law of fear and bondage. Under it man was God's servant and the Synagogue was only teacher and taskmaster. But since God has given us His Son, all that is changed. Now God is our Father; our home, then, is heaven; our inheritance is all that God owns and all that God is! And the Church, far from being merely a teacher and a taskmaster, is now a loving and holy Mother who nourishes her children of God for God and lovingly leads them home.

But all that does not take away our toys! We are still children, the oldest of us — and we can become so absorbed in the toys of time that we can forget our Mother and even be unmindful of our Father. We can lose ourselves so completely in them that we lose not only Christmas Day and the Christmas season but even the endless day of eternity and the very Christ! That is why God is urgent now at this point in your spelling; that is why there is weeping and wailing in Rama and why Rachel will not be comforted; that is why some innocent children were slain and the Child who was and is God was carried off into exile. God must alert us to many truths, not the least of which is that His Christmas greeting and gift become the Gospel which tells us that our goal ultimately is to bear *witness to the Truth!*

THEY ARE
ONLY TOYS

L
G-O-D
V
E

101

Hence we are not to lose ourselves in toys. We are to pray
as Louise Guiney prayed in her poem *Deo Optimo Maximo:*

Delight is a menace, if Thou brood not by;
Power is a quicksand; *Fame,* a gathering jeer.

Oft as the morn (though none of earth deny
These three are dear)
Wash me of them,

That I may be renewed and wander free,
And wander free amid my new-born joys.

Close Thou my hand upon Beatitude,
Not on her *toys!*

God is your beatitude. The things of time are toys. You
are eternity's child and your eternity has already begun! There
is a compelling urgency to every day and every hour of the
day. In it we are to witness to the truth — that God greeted
and gifted us at Christmas.

If you know what witness means, you understand why
God brings St. Stephen, St. John, and the Holy Innocents to
the crib in the cave as soon as Christ is born liturgically.
To be a witness is to be a *martyr.* Holy Mother Church wishes
us to realize that we were born in baptism to become *Christ*
— He who was the world's outstanding Martyr. Therefore,
we, if we will be true to our calling, will become martyrs
either like St. Stephen, that is by both will and act; or like
St. John, in will only, not in act; or, for the young among us,
like the Innocents, in act and not in will.

Baptism was a birth of a new Christ; therefore a Christmas
Day. St. Augustine teaches that clearly when he says: "A
Christian is another *Christ.*" Baptism, however, was the birthday not of a noble being, but of one who would live by a
life that is divine! Hence the sacrament is an initiation not
only into holiness, but into heroic holiness; for it is an initiation
into the very holiness of God. God's gift to you is nothing

L
G-O-D
V
E

102

less than God Himself. You are to live with His life; you are to witness to His truth. That is why you have come into this world. Remember that time, that precious commodity which so many squander so recklessly, is a creature of God that is flung against a background of eternity. Its each split second can purchase an eternity of happiness with God or unending hate and unendurable unhappiness in hell. Its each passing moment demands that you witness to the truth of Christ — or you, unwittingly perhaps, will witness to the awful truth of antichrist.

God is speaking to you — and speaking with tremendous earnestness and urgency. With the loud lamentation of Rachel breaking on your ear God says: "Life is a warfare. Earth is a battleground. You are a wayfarer, an exile, a prodigal far from your home; you are nevertheless a soldier of Jesus Christ and a member of the Church Militant."

Those strident statements are to alert you. They do not mean that you are to give up your toys but only that you are to recognize them as toys; and while you are to enjoy them, you are not to make them your life. You have beatitude before you. It can be attained only by one of the three kinds of martyrdom, each of which calls for living in Christ Jesus!

Leon Bloy, when once asked what he was bringing his children up to be, replied like a flash: "Martyrs." A baptized person has no other goal in life; for he is to witness to the truth of Christ by making his life a Mass — and Mass is the perfect martyrdom! Your martyrdom need not be as red as was the Christ's, nor as brutal as was Stephen's, nor as brief as was the Innocents. You, like John, may know a long, long life, which is, undoubtedly, the hardest of all hard martyrdoms. But if you are to return God's greeting at Christmas, you must be a martyr. There is no way out.

What clever contrast God uses to bolster your courage in the face of life's hard fact! In this Flight into Egypt, which looks like consummate weakness, is God's proof that there

L

G-O-D

V

E

103

is no strength on earth but His. Herod was a despot who had tyrannized over Judea for almost forty years. Pit Joseph, Mary, and the Child against Herod's trained mercenaries. Think of all the avenues of information Herod had; yet he never knew when, nor exactly where, the Christ was born. And Jesus was off in Egypt with Mary and Joseph while this powerful despot rotted amidst a cringing court, and finally died without ever having touched the Child.

You are Christ. What have you to fear from the mighty of this world? Tyrants and toys should make you smile and have you joyfully returning God's Christmas greeting.

God wants you to go down into Egypt to learn that even in His most urgent message He has put joy.

EGYPT
SPEAKS

Egypt is a land that can teach you much about toys; for countless are the little and great of mankind who have played with them here. Since few can think of Egypt without thinking of the Pyramids and the Sphinx, the Great Pyramid, which in its way is a monument to toys, can serve as the focus of your reflections. The great Pyramid was erected fully two thousand years before Abram, off in Ur of the Chaldees, heard that momentous word of God: "Go forth out of thy country . . . and I will make of thee a great nation" (Gen. 12:1-2). Since Abram heard and believed that word two thousand years before Christ was born, you of the twentieth century are at least six thousand years away from the building of this Great Pyramid. Yet, before its first huge block was laid, civilizations had already known maturity and complete decline. Hence mankind was old when Abram made his way into Egypt. Sumerians and Akkadians had already played with toys — and never knew, perhaps, what trifles they were. In Christ's time Egyptians, Babylonians, Assyrians, Hittites, and Minoans were still playing with them — most likely in the same ignorance.

L
G-O-D
V
E

If, at the time of Abram, one had been asked which of these highly developed and solidly established societies would exercise the greatest influence on the future of mankind, he would have been hard put to make a prediction. For Egypt had a genius for organization; Minoan Crete had commercial wealth and maritime flexibility; while Babylon had developed an elaborate economy, and Assyria had a naked and even savage aggressiveness. Yet, if one living then could have seen with the eyes of God — as you can now with hindsight — he would pass over these powers with their wealth and skills, and look on Abram with his tiny clan of Thare. This insignificant handful was to influence most deeply all subsequent history and every son of man, because they were God's Chosen People — as you are!

It is more than reassuring to gaze at the Great Pyramid and realize that before this structure was so much as dreamed of, God was thinking of you and your Christmas. To remember that Abram once looked on the same monument is to have your trust in the might of God renewed and your perception of the toylike quality in the power of men refreshed. For, had you lived two thousand years before Christ, you would have been forced to name as the most insignificant group on earth Abram and his tribe of Thare. Yet two thousand years after Christ, you know them to have been God's most significant handful, the only group that truly influenced the future and whose descendants have great impact even in the present day.

Their presence in the twentieth century should tell certain historians that when they talk about "the inexorable law of recurrence" which governs races and cultures and even religions, and teach that each civilization has "its seasons" and every people their "growth and decline" they are talking and teaching nonsense. There is only one law of history, as Abram in the presence of the Great Pyramid reminds us. It is the irresistible will of God. That is the way the Chosen People viewed history: not as conditioned recurrence but as the progressive unfolding of God's plan for man. Against

L
G-O-D
V
E

all experience and all apparent reason, these people maintained with an obstinate faith that the God of high heaven had chosen them to declare to the world the truth that history had a meaning, and that meaning was contained in the destiny of their own race. This single pastoral people of a few thousand souls had the message of all messages for mankind; they had to tell that there would be a Christmas! They had to teach that the things of time are toys.

Jesus, Mary, and Joseph fled into Egypt — to teach you that your God is the living and true God; that all men, no matter what their might, are His weak creatures who are working out His will. God wants you to know that you are in exile. He is anxious as He speaks; for He knows how alluring His world can be. But He wants you to realize it is your place of exile, your land of Egypt. But if this wondrous world is only your place of exile, what must your native land be like? If you can have the pleasure of God's voice and God's close companionship, if you can be His member while on the road home, what will you be when you arrive? If this be the night of life, what will the dawn and the day bring? If all this beauty be but shadow, what, oh what will the Substance be?

Egypt is speaking to you of your eternal Jerusalem.

But remember why Joseph and Mary took the Child into the land of the Pyramids and the Sphinx. *His hour had not yet come!* The Paschal Lamb must grow to the perfection demanded for the Holocaust.

You are celebrating a birthday. But God brings in a deathday in the midst of your celebration. He would teach you that you are to be prudent while in exile. You are to flee when necessary so that you may be alive with grace when your hour comes — the hour He has appointed from the beginning to be the hour when you should go Home.

The Christ Child, thanks to His foster father and His loving Mother, used proper means to attain His proper end.

L
G-O-D
V
E

106

When the land of the Chosen People grew inimical to His life, He went into a pagan land so that He might be ready when God's hour struck.

Every hour in your life, of course, is God's hour; and you are to use every proper means to achieve God's end in each hour. You are to give Him glory every moment of every hour by being victorious over His enemies and yours. This will often necessitate flight into Egypt; for you must save the life of the Child within you until God's appointed hour for consummation. PRUDENCE WILL WIN OVER ALL

God is speaking to you with earnestness and urgency, for He wants you to know that your deathday will be your true birthday and that your birthday by baptism was the day on which you were given the assignment to live for Christ and one day to die for Him as did the Innocents. God is giving you "a reason to live and a reason to die." That reason is He whose birth you celebrate at Christmas.

What consolation there is for you in the fact that you will be born to eternal life at the moment an infinitely loving God has decreed. If necessary, He will send an angel to your parents or to you to save you for that blessed hour — that hour of your *Ite, Missa Est* — the completion of your Mass.

An ex-Communist has said that he was leaving the winning side when he quit the Communists, the enemies of Christ. But the facts of history tell you the opposite. There is only one side that wins — God's side. And you are on it! In St. Peter's Square in Rome there stands a stone column that was once in the Circus Maximus of Nero. Cut deep into its heart are the words: *Christus Vivit. Christus Regnat. Christus Imperat.* Loosely, they can be translated: "Christ alone wins!" And at Christmas God is greeting and presenting you with Christ!

"Out of Egypt have I called my Son" is the Scripture that was to be fulfilled. It is found in the first verse of Osee's eleventh chapter. There we learn that Israel, the Chosen

L
G-O-D
V
E

107

People of God, were punished for their ingratitude by exile into Egypt. But God, who is love, speaks through the mouth of the Prophet saying: "Because Israel was a child and I loved him: and I called my son out of Egypt." You know whither He called Israel. It was to the Promised Land. Those people were but a figure of Christ, the only-begotten Son who was to be called out of Egypt — ultimately to the everlasting Promised Land!

You are in Egypt! God will one day call you into your Promised Land — if you are prudent all the days of your exile and flee when flight is called for!

Do not forget that Egypt was the land of the Paschal Lamb. Jesus had to go there; for He is the true Paschal Lamb, who was called out of Egypt to save by saying Mass.

The parallel is clear: you are in Egypt. God will one day call you out for the same purpose He called the true Paschal Lamb. It will be to say your Mass! You will say it as triumphantly as did the Christ — if you are prudent enough to make use of all the means God puts at your disposal to be a veritable Jesus!

God is telling you that life on earth is filled with urgency but there is no need to fear. Against worldly wisdom, the deceits of the Flesh and the Devil there is an impregnable armor — holy prudence, that theological gift which God gave you at baptism. Use it and one day God will call you out of Egypt to be witness to the truth that He has loved you with an everlasting love.

See how God resolves the discord? See how joyful His greeting really is? The black was only for contrast; the discord only to emphasize the magnificence of the melody.

God is telling you that though you are in exile you are ever a citizen of the Holy City of God; that though Paradise has been lost by the first Adam, this Second Adam, who was carried into Egypt, has made it possible for you to have a Garden of Eden in your heart. You are in exile — but your

L
G-O-D
V
E

heaven has already begun. You are in time, yet your eternity is going on! You are to win your way to God, yet God comes to you in every event of your day and night, in every breath you breathe and every beat of your heart.

God is saying that while you are surrounded by tyrants worse than Herod, you will always escape their swords if you but listen to His angels and do His bidding.

Now let us finish our spelling of the Word.

L
G-O-D
V
E

CHRIST AMONG THE DOCTORS
BY MATTHIAS STOMER
BAYERISCHE STAATSGEMAELDESAMMLUNGEN. MUNICH

S-A-V-I-O-U-R

Return and Retirement Reveal the Riches of Life in God's Word

R is the final letter in the word God uses to greet you at Christmas. It completes your slow spelling out of "Saviour." It stands, as you might well guess, for the return to Nazareth — both after His Flight into Egypt and the Finding in the Temple. It has to do with retirement, in which you are to discover the riches hidden in God's word.

St. Matthew has the account of the Flight, the Slaughter of the Innocents, and the Return crowded into a few verses of his short second chapter. Rachel is still weeping and will not be comforted, it seems, when an angel again shakes Joseph in his sleep.

> In due time after the death of Herod, an angel of the Lord appeared in a dream to Joseph in Egypt and said: "Rise! Take with you the child and his mother, and set out for the land of Israel. They who were plotting against the life of the Child are dead."(Mt. 2:19, 20.)*

See how futile it is to fight against God! See how exactly all prophecies are fulfilled. Herod dies. "Out of Egypt have I called My Son" is immediately put into action. Do you not hear your God pleading with you as He greets you, begging that you have absolute trust, complete and entire confidence in Him? You are Christ — Heaven will take as much care

---

*Kleist-Lilly translation.

111

of you unto your predestined hour as it did of Jesus. There is no room for fear in those who live in Christ. Yet there must always be ample room for *temperance*.

> He [Joseph] rose and, taking the child and his mother with him, returned to the land of Israel. But when he learned that Archelaus had succeeded his father Herod as king of Judea, he was afraid to go there; so, after being advised in a dream, he withdrew to the province of Galilee. Thither he went, making his home in a town called Nazareth; that so might be fulfilled the prediction made through the prophets, that he was to be called a Nazarene. (Mt. 2:21–23.)*

It seems quite certain that Joseph planned to return to Bethlehem and there take up his abode with his wife, who was Mother of God, and his God who would call him "Father." What could have been more natural? Had not even Caesar Augustus made Joseph highly conscious that he was a son of David, and that Bethlehem was his ancestral seat? Can you not hear Mary telling him all the prophecies concerning the Child of her womb and their references to David and Bethlehem? What else would they talk about when in exile? Did it not seem God's plan? Had not heaven and earth combined to bring them from Galilee to Judea for His birth? What else could the decree from Rome be but God's will and God's way of having His only Son come forth in the little town that was known to all as "David's Town"? But it was at Gaza, most likely, as they gaily came back, that they heard that Archelaus was reigning over Judea. That gave Joseph pause, and clouded the gay skies for the Holy Family.

This was probably the gayest trip the Holy Family ever had — except perhaps the other Mystery we are contemplating in this chapter — the First Ascent to Jerusalem, when Jesus was twelve. The trip from Nazareth to Bethlehem when Mary was still with Child was too fraught with anxiety on Joseph's part about the condition of his wife for it to be pleasant.

L
G-O-D
V
E

*Kleist-Lilly translation.

The Flight into Egypt was anything but pleasant, as you have seen. But this return was all gaiety — until they arrived at Gaza. With what a different feeling Joseph must have awakened Mary after hearing from the angel that Herod was dead and that they were to go back "to the land of Israel." With what an utterly different emotion Mary must have gathered the Babe in her arms! And how Jesus Himself, with that knowledge that was His as God, must have rejoiced to be fulfilling another prophecy for the Father: "Out of Egypt . . ."

"Out of Egypt . . ." You can be sure that every mile was short and every hour brief as they left the land of the Nile and re-entered the desert. Even this barren waste must have had a golden hue about it for the holy travelers. That is the way God would have every life lived: in joy! The exultant joy that comes from pleasing Him, from loving Him by doing His holy will.

Can you not imagine the plans Joseph outlined for Mary as they came across the desert sands? He would set up shop at Bethlehem. There would be work aplenty there. He would see to it that their little house was cozy. He would build a special crib for the Boy and make sure that He had plenty of things to play with. And Mary, you can be sure, was filled with the happiest anticipation. It was a trip brim full with tenderness — until they came to Gaza.

"Out of Egypt . . ." They had come with the same promptness they had gone into Egypt. But when they were told that Archelaus was reigning in Judea, Joseph paused. It might not be safe for Jesus; for more than likely Archelaus shared his father's fear of anyone pretending to be Messias or claiming the title of King. There might well be another slaughter of innocents if Archelaus heard that Jesus was back.

Then once again in a dream Joseph heard from heaven. Joseph's decision to go back to Nazareth must not have been an unpleasant one to make. It is true they were only two

HEAVEN
SPEAKS
AGAIN

113

easy days travel from Bethlehem, while Nazareth was far to the north; but Nazareth was ever so much more "home" to both Joseph and Mary than Bethlehem had ever been! Yet the Child was to be considered. His future . . . Ah, but could they not leave that in the hands of God? So north they turned. Across Ascalon, Ashdod, and Caesarea. After that the road was straight. They went through the pass of Megeddo, crossed the lovely, history-laden plain of Esdelon, and finally reached home.

Matthew tells us this was to fulfill a prediction made through the prophets — that Jesus would be called a Nazarene. But scholars have scanned the prophets without once finding such a prediction. Yet we know only too well that Jesus *was* called a Nazarene! Nathaniel had a sneer for the town, you may remember. Most likely, he was but quoting an old saying when he asked: "Can anything good come out of Nazareth?" We also know that official Rome had this title placed upon Christ's cross so that for all time He will be known as Jesus of Nazareth. Moreover, His early followers were called "Nazarenes," and even today by Jews and Moslems the same title is given the followers of Mary's Son. St. Jerome, and most Catholic commentators after him, give the explanation that Matthew is referring in general here to the Messianic prophecies, and not to any one prophet or prophecy. The trend of the predictions about the Messias show Him to be One who would be scorned, as are those from some despised province or town. Jesus was born at Bethlehem and made Capharnaum His center during His Public Life, but for happiness on earth and for the holiest of holy abodes in the world we have to go to Nazareth and see Jesus, Mary, and Joseph as a Family.

GOD SEEMED
ORDINARY

One word will characterize perfectly what you will see there. And it shows you the very source of the joy that is proper to Christmas and the entire life of a Christian. That word is *ordinary*.

NAZARETH
BY FRANCOIS LE FOND
FOUND IN THE CHURCH OF ST. JOSEPH, NAZARETH

In this house at Nazareth Jesus is to spend thirty of His thirty-three years of life. His Immaculate Mother will be with Him every moment. And here the just Joseph will live and die. That means that you have before your eyes a house that holds God, the Mother of God, and the man closest to Christ. Obviously it is far holier than the very Holy of Holies up in Jerusalem.

Ordinary seems a strange word to use about the most extraordinary Family that ever lived on our earth. Yet it is gospel truth. St. Luke summarizes the first twelve years of Christ's life in the lines:

> The Child grew strong in body and soul as his intelligence developed; and the grace of God rested upon him. (Lk. 2:40.)*

Of the eighteen years after the Finding in the Temple the same Evangelist writes:

> He went down in their company and came to Nazareth, where he was subject to them. . . . And Jesus made steady progress, proportionately to his age, in understanding and in favor with God and men. (Lk. 2:51, 52.)*

Study those lines closely and you will learn that the largest part of God's life on earth was most ordinary. Of the vast majority of boys it could be written: "He grew strong in body and soul as his intelligence developed." And would not most parents say of their sons: "He was subject to us — and made steady progress, proportionately to his age, in understanding and favor . . ."? Yet those are the very phrases that tell you how the Son of God grew to manhood. More than that, they tell you how for thirty full years He glorified God. Now there is the all-important point: Jesus was on earth for the very same purpose you and I have been placed here — to glorify the Father. He did it, and did it perfectly, by so ordinary a life that when, in His thirty-first year, He began to manifest Himself to the world, the people in whose midst He had lived for three full decades were shocked and even scan-

L
G-O-D
V
E

---

* Kleist-Lilly translation.

115

dalized. When He began to teach and preach, they exclaimed: "Is not this man the son of the carpenter? . . . And his mother, is not Mary her name?" (Lk. 13:55, 56.) They knew Him with that thoroughness only the people of tiny villages can know one another. They had seen Him grow from babyhood to boyhood, and then on to manhood. They had watched Him play, at first, in Joseph's shop; then gradually learn His father's trade; and finally, take over from that father and become the village carpenter. It had been all so ordinary, and He had appeared so plain and ordinary, that for Him to ascend the pulpit was scandal itself.

But all that ordinariness is to inspire you. Christ's Hidden Life holds the thrilling truth that you can become like Christ in what everyone considers, and what actually is, *ordinary*. For Jesus, who was and is God, would never waste a single moment of time while He was on earth. He Himself testifies that He "always did the things that pleased the Father." That means that Nazareth, with its thirty years so filled with the ordinary, fits into the great drama of the Redemption as no unimportant part. It means that He, who was "the first-born of many brethren," was saving those brethren by these years at Nazareth just as really, though far less dramatically, as by the three tragic hours on Golgotha. That is the truth the holy Council of Trent teaches when it declares that the eighteen hours of Christ's Passion and Death were the principal — but not the only — part of His Redemption. That precisely, is the climaxing point God would make as He greets you at Christmas. It is as if He would say: "My Son, by becoming an ordinary human being, redeemed mankind; you, an ordinary human being, can become like My Son, and help complete mankind's salvation."

L
G-O-D
V
E

There is the joy of the Christian, and of Christmas: You have been saved; for on this day there was "born to you a Saviour, who is Christ the Lord" — and you, by being born again in Christ the Lord *can become a Saviour*, too!

There is God's greeting — His gift — His Gospel — and your goal. Can you be other than merry? And remember the stress is on *ordinary*.

But to God "ordinary" does not mean mediocre. For in His Kingdom there is no room for the mediocre. He told us that Himself when, with something close to violence, He spoke to the Laodiceans and said: "I know your conduct. You are not cold, you are not hot. Would that you were cold or hot! And so, because you are lukewarm and neither cold nor hot, I am going to vomit you out of my mouth" (Apoc. 3:15, 16).*

To God, "ordinary" does not mean lukewarm, nor what moderns term normal or natural; for once you have been baptized you have ceased to be natural! And most moderns seem to mean "negligible" when they speak of a thing being "normal." God means none of these when He insists that since His Son, true God of true God, became an ordinary human, ordinary humans are to become Godlike. Perhaps it will clarify the point to say God means *usual*. He means that you are to live your usual day, do your duties, meet your problems, greet your callers in your usual manner. He would have you be as you usually are, but for the one purpose which should be usual with you — *the glory of God* and the *good of men*.

Life cannot be the same once you have been greeted by God. Life cannot be the same once you have been baptized. For after baptism, as was said above, you ceased to be natural, purely human, normal, ordinary, or usual in the common acceptance of those words. You became a human-divine being; you became extraordinary because supernatural! Hence to live up to your new nature you can never be natural or just human! And that is precisely the point in God's greeting: you have been *saved* — for "There is born to you a Saviour who is Christ the Lord." But now ask yourself: *From what have you been saved?*

---

* Kleist-Lilly translation.

L
G-O-D
V
E

SAVED FROM WHAT?

Not from sickness, suffering, sorrow, or death. You are going to know each of those intimately. Perhaps some of them will be your companions all your life long. So the Babe of Bethlehem did not save you from any of these. Nor did He save you from harassing temptation. That you will meet in some form every day, and perhaps every hour of the day. And since Proverbs has its dictum about the "just man falling seven times," it is clear that you have not been saved from sin.

Yet the heart of God's Christmas greeting and His gift is the fact that "there was born to you a *Saviour*." From what did He save?

Not from those things of time that mortals dread, but from something we immortals do not dread enough. He saved you from an eternity without God! He saved you from hell. He saved you from everlasting frustration and endless despair. He saved you from the torment of gnawing, but never consuming, *hate*. He saved you from the torture of having a mind that craves truth, but is never able to possess it; from the agony of having a will that ever reaches out for good, but is never able to grasp it. He saved you from the inexpressible hell of not loving God!

But right here on earth, and in ever passing time, God by this greeting has saved you from agonies that can break hearts and minds and souls. He has given you a Gospel and a goal — there are millions who have neither! He has given you a reason to live and a reason to die — hundreds of millions go on existing without either. He has given you the ability to grasp substance, while others can only grope and touch shadow and semblance. He has given you a philosophy of life which is really a theology of eternity. He has saved you from so much that it will take you all eternity to grasp the world of truth contained in the line "There is born to you a *Saviour*."

Think now on what He has saved you *for*. Briefly, He has saved you for *happiness*. That is why God wishes you a

L
G-O-D
V
E

118

Merry Christmas. And God repeats this greeting not only annually, but daily, because He would have you know that you are made for happiness here as well as hereafter. That is the meaning of Christmas — of Christ — and of Christianity.

There is no man, woman, or child on this earth of ours who is not seeking but one thing — happiness. The child with its nose pressed against the window filled with Christmas toys is seeking exactly the same thing as the miner in the depths of the earth who is picking away for gold or diamonds or uranium. The woman who seeks dominance in society or fame as a leader in thought is searching for exactly the same thing as the teen-ager who craves flashy socks and a permanent wave. To these persons these things bring a temporary satisfaction; so it is clear that it is *happiness* they are seeking through these things. But only those who know Christ Jesus know the source of the happiness which does not fade; and only those who have heard God's greeting and accepted His gift, know Christ Jesus. So it is correct to say He has saved you *from* frustration and *for* complete satisfaction; *from* seeing truth only in a twilight and *for* possessing it in Light Inaccessible; *from* the futility of handling this good and that and *for* the joy of possessing all good; *from* the feverishness of experimental searching and *for* the calm of steady progressive finding; *from* the weariness of tasting this and that pleasure and *for* the joy that ever rejuvenates; *from* the ceaseless anxiety that underlies all drifting with tides and being a plaything of winds, and *for* the comfort that comes from a strong steady rudder steering one to a known and definite port.

"There is born to you a Saviour — who is Christ the Lord." Although it will take eternity to plumb the depths of meaning in that line, we can realize this little bit today: God has saved you from stumbling in darkness and enabled you to walk in the light! From the moment you began to live humanly, that is, from the moment you began to think and will and walk toward some goal, you have had need of

L
G-O-D
V
E

119

truth, the light by which all rational beings walk. But you can look around you Christmas Day and see millions who are not really walking no matter how brisk their step may be; they are stumbling; they are blind; and they are being led by the blind — because they know not that a Saviour is born to them. They have not heard what you have heard: God's Christmas greeting. Do you see what God has saved you from and what He has saved you for? *From* being at best the most intelligent of animals, and *for* at worst being at least God's prodigal child. *From* being at best a highly cultured human, and *for* being at least the densest and dumbest of the divine!

"There is born to you a Saviour," to save you from unhappiness in time and eternity and for the delight of being like unto *God* every moment of your existence on earth and in the endlessness of the life beyond earth!

God has gifted you with *Him* who is Light and Truth, with *Him* who is Goodness and Beauty, with *Him* who is the Living Life. God has gifted you with Jesus Christ — and you must not only return His greeting but His gift as well. For you must *be* Christ Jesus!

Seven letters are in God's word. Seven gifts are given with that word. And seven virtues are infused at your "Christmas" — your birth into Christ and Christ's birth into you by grace. You see now that God's greeting is the very gift of Himself through His Son. You are to return God's greeting by making a gift of yourself to Him.

You Are the One for Whom
Love Does Such Things!

Now, perhaps as never before, you know that God became man in order to *save* and that He did it by the *Mass*. You know His mission was to save all men; and He accomplished that mission magnificently. All *are* redeemed. He founded a Church, one whose doors are open to all; for it is the one visible means God instituted through which all men may be *saved*. Yet, you must have sensed the paradox of it all as you went through these pages; for God has been speaking to *you*, second person singular, the often isolated and lonely individual that is *yourself*.

God did not become man, nor did He found His Church for any vague generality. God really knows only the individual. With Him, and with His Church, it is always the solitary soul which is the possession and eternal responsibility of the single person. Hence God's Christmas greeting is directed to *you*. You are to be as self-conscious as was the great and generous St. Paul, who was dominated by the one all-powerful and all-pervasive idea: *Dilexit me — et tradidit semitipsum pro me —* "He [God] loved *me —* and gave Himself up for *me*." The personal pronoun is personal — and meant to be so by your personal God.

The same is true of His Church. For that is not only His voice, but His very Word. It is the Mystical Body of His

121

Christ, His Anointed One. But you know bodies are always in the possession of a person. That is why you can say simply and truly: The Church is Christ. You need not be surprised, then, to note that this Church, this one and only universal Church, this Church for all men of all times and all places, is a Church that is concerned ever with the individual. The pope in Rome, each of his cardinals, every single archbishop, bishop, prelate, and priest, is filled with concern for the individual. It is the single soul of each that they want to save; it is the individual human being with all his potentialities to be divine that concerns them. Of course it is the Word for whom they live; yet He is a Word who cannot live on earth without His syllables — His individual, separate, single syllables.

Needless to say, Christ's hierarchy, from Supreme Pontiff to latest ordained priest, has grave concern for the general good of the universal Church and of all men. Listen to any Christmas message of the pope, or of any prelate, pastor, or curate, and you will learn how universal is their concern. Yet as you listen more closely you will realize that each member of this teaching and governing body of the Church is keenly conscious that there is a reciprocal relation between the whole and its parts; that the good of the whole depends on the good of the individuals who make up that whole. So the focus is really on the individual. For while the Church has machinery, it is not a machine; while it boasts an organization, it is really an organism; it lives and breathes and moves in its members — the ones who run the machinery and keep up the organization. The individual will ever be the prime concern. Such is the will of God. Christ, you have seen, was for the Mass — and the Mass is for the individual souls of men. Your soul and my soul. What things does Love do!

Just as Mary's Son was not concerned with mankind but with men, so His vicar, the reigning pontiff, will not be concerned with Russia, but with individual Russians; not with

L
G-O-D
V
E

122

the Americas but with each individual American; not with the world of people but with the separate and single persons of the world. For Christ came not for the flock, but for the individual sheep — especially the strays. With God and His Son, and with the Church that Son founded, it was, is, and ever will be the individual that counts. So God's greeting at Christmas is not for your family so much as for *you*.

Now the realization will gradually dawn that God's greeting to you has not been fully explained at all; that you have but scratched the surface of the many mysteries involved; that what God is really saying is: "The best is yet to be!"

After learning that Divine Providence is not that vague, impersonal governance of the world that you thought it was, but the hand of God in your hand, and the heart of God in all your interests; after learning that angels are all about you: over yourself, your family, your Church, town, city, state, and nation; after learning that these angels have annunciations for you from God — all of which are for the purpose of asking your *Fiat* so that God might take flesh in you; it seems impossible that the best is yet to be. Still, that is precisely what God is saying.

Despite the fact that you know now, more clearly than ever before, that Jesus is *your* Jesus; that a cave was hollowed out and a crib shaped; that Caesar Augustus was prompted to enroll the whole world, just that your Jesus might be born in Bethlehem; after watching the Virgin who had conceived without losing her virginity go up into the hill country and tell her relatives about the Might and Mercy who is your God; after listening to oblations being made that meant the sundering of the bolts and bars of heaven; after seeing how your God saves individuals for His hour and fills them with joy as they live in retirement awaiting His high and holy hour — after all that, it does seem difficult to believe that anything better is yet to be. Still, that is what God says.

He gave you a mind that could know Him, the Great

L

G-O-D

V

E

123

Invisible, from looking at the visible things of His world. It is a gift that sets you as crown to His wondrous visible creation. But that was not enough for you or for Him. So He widened the horizons of the intellectual world for you by giving you a new light — the Light of Faith. This enables you to see into the invisible world of God, and know something of His mysteries. He had given you a heart with which to love the good and take to that heart the beautiful. He had dowered you with a will that was strong and free. Yet, though He had gifted you as no other creature on earth, He was not satisfied. He had made you in His own image and likeness. But even that was not enough for His love. He would have you share His very Being. That is why Christ came. That is why there was a Christmas. And yet God tells you "the *best* is yet to be."

When you were a child a toy could fill your whole being with gladness. You were filled; never forget it. But as you grew, the toy was tossed aside and some other thing filled your soul. Have you yourself not noted how the object of your desires changed with the passage of the years? As you grew older, you demanded things challenging and intimate to satisfy you. In youth it was most likely a friend. Then came the desire for a mate. As life went on, your object may have become success in your particular field — and you may have achieved it. But you were no more filled with happiness than when you had been a child. You will go into old age, enjoy leisure, and look at life with wiser eyes and far less greedy heart. You will love more deeply, with greater satisfaction and far less unrest. So at every stage, though you thought you had known contentment, you could have said what God is saying this moment. You could have said: "The best is yet to be." And even in old age you can look beyond the last horizon and know that God has saved something better than anything you have known. He has really saved the *best;* for He has saved an eternity that will be one long Christmas —

L
G-O-D
V
E

124

since you will see face to face Him who is the Christ and was the Mass!

So when God greets you at Christmas, He is talking of more than the present. He is also telling you about that endless future which we call eternity. He is telling you that you will not only see the Babe of Bethlehem face to face but you will come to know His Mother, that Maid of Nazareth who became your Mother during His Mass. You will see those angels who sundered the heavens above Bethlehem and at first frightened, then charmed the shepherds with the very glory of God. You will live forever with John the Baptist, his mother Elizabeth, and the man who gave us the stirring *Benedictus*. You will be an associate of all those who have shed their blood for the Child, from the handful of Holy Innocents to the hoards of men and women now winning martyrdom under Chinese and Russian Reds. You will come to know everyone whom God has loved with a special love and who have returned that love very specially. All this — if you return God's greeting and accept God's gift. Indeed the best is yet to be.

At Christmas many parents are troubled about the morality of perpetuating the idea of Santa Claus. The problem is easily solved; there *is* a Santa Claus. His name is *God*. Not Kriss Kringle. Not St. Nicholas. The real Santa Claus is He who gave life to Kriss Kringle and to all who believe in that Dutch version of the Christmas story. It is He who inspired St. Nicholas not only with sanctity, but with the idea of being loving and joyful enough to stuff stockings with presents on the birthday of his Lord and yours.

Why not tell yourself and your children the truth? Tell them that God is Santa Claus, and that the greatest Gift He could ever give was given this day. Tell them that every greeting they hear or give of "Merry Christmas" is but the echo of God's Word. That every gift they receive, every present they wrap, is but symbol and memento of Him who

L
G-O-D
V
E

125

was given us by God as gift, and wrapped by Mary in swaddling clothes. Tell them that He who is the Truth makes Christmas and makes it merry. Make it plain to them that there is a Christmas only because there is a Christ and there is a Mass!

Teach your children that this is a feast of forty days; that it is a season just like Lent, Advent, Easter, or Pentecost; that it runs from December 25 to February 2. You can go through the mysteries with them as you have just done in these pages. Show them that Mary brings the forty-day period to a close by presenting Him in the Temple for the Offertory of His Mass. Stress for them the fact that "Christmas" is made up of "Christ" and "Mass."

As they grow, they should learn that they celebrate Christmas on December 25 for very sound historical reasons. Give them the gospel truths about that Census the Emperor of Rome demanded, which brought Joseph and Mary to Bethlehem. Point out that the early Church of Rome had access to these Public Records and could have no difficulty in ascertaining the date of His birth. Give them the argument from Sacred Scripture. It is easily deduced from the fact that Zachary had his vision of Gabriel in the "seventh month," the month of *Tisri,* which corresponds to the end of our September and the beginning of our October. Count for them the six intervening months to bring them to March and the angel's Annunciation to Mary which ended with Gabriel's telling her that Elizabeth was six months along with child. Tell them that if Mary said *Fiat* on March 25, as we claim, then Jesus was born on the very date we celebrate as His birthday — December 25.

They will be interested in hearing that Christmas is fixed to this one date for some wonderful reasons. Easter and Good Friday, those other two days that mean so much to your children — and to the Christ Child — are movable: they change every year. But Christmas, like the Annunciation, is

L
G-O-D
V
E

126

always on the twenty-fifth of the month. They will be impressed when you tell them it is believed that God made man on Friday and saved Him on the same day; that God made light rise over the world on a Sunday, and that is why He Himself rose from the dead as the Light of the World on a Sunday; but for the day of the birth of the One who was to save and sanctify no one day could be assigned — for every day is to be sanctified and every day sinners are to be saved!

You can put it all in the form of an acrostic they will never forget by arranging five wonderful words in this fashion:

L

Mary   G - O - D   *Mass*

V

E

Christ

Tell them that God's greeting at Christmas is like Himself — it is all love. It came to us first in the form of an Infant at Bethlehem; it was seen last as a Corpse on a criminal's Cross. For the Son of God and the Son of Mary offered Mass for us by stretching wide His hands as the Crucified. That is why the arrangement of the words in this cruciform, when rightly understood, tells all there is to tell about God, about life, about love, and about themselves.

God is the heart of the monogram; for God is the heart of all that matters. But who knows God, or what God is? St. John the Evangelist sought and sought for words that would tell the truth about God; and he sought in vain until the Spirit of Truth came upon him, and he wrote: *Deus Caritas Est* — "God is Love" (1 Jn. 4:16).

In the acrostic the two words are so entwined that they are formed from the one substance, with the vowel "O" as the heart of both words. This will suggest to your children that when one has said "God is Love" one has said all that

L

G-O-D

V

E

need be said about God. But you can tell them something more about love.

Love gives. True love is never satisfied until it has given its very self; God, the Perfect Lover, was not satisfied until He had given Himself. He did not rest until the Divine and the human were locked in such an embrace that we say "the Word became flesh and dwelt amongst us." The God of heaven was so deeply in love with us that He became *Emmanuel* — one with us.

With those two lessons learned they can be told about the words outside the cross.

Mary is one of us, yet so limitlessly above us that St. Thomas of Aquin, that Angel of the Schools, tells us she "borders on the Infinite." That is why she is placed in line with God. She was His handmaid through whom His Christ came to us. Mother of God, she became Mother of all men when she practically said Mass with her Son, compassionating Him in His Passion and Co-redeeming with Him in His Redemption. She made Christmas possible by giving us the Christ.

Christ stands at the center of the monogram because He stands at the center of all time and all true history. He is the heart of that wondrous science of theology which begins by telling of the unbeginning God and goes on until it has told of the Four Last Things. In this design He is placed below God not because He is not God, but because, being God and being Love, "He emptied Himself," came down to earth, "taking the nature of a slave, fashioned as He was in the likeness of man and recognized by outward appearance as a man" (Phil. 2:7).

Out of love God became man that in love He might climb the cross and make of it an altar on which to say His first Mass. He offered that Mass that men might be lifted up to the very level of God, share in His nature, live with His life even while here on earth, be made God's very children and legitimate heirs to His heaven.

L
G-O-D
V
E

Mass is placed on a line with God because, strictly speaking, only God could or can say Mass. It is an infinite thing — a Sacrifice in which God is both Offerer and Offering, Priest and Victim, Giver of the Infinite Gift and that Gift's Infinite Receiver. The Mass is of God and for God — it is perfect reparation of His outraged infinity. But it is also for you — and is to be of you. The word rests on the same line with "God" and "Mary" to show that we children of Mary and children of God can go back to our Father and Mother only through the Mass: *Per Ipsum, et cum Ipso, et in Ipso* "Through Him and with Him and in Him" — the Babe of Bethlehem, who became Christ in order to say Mass. We have become Christians for no other purpose.

You explain God's greeting rightly only when you tell yourself and your children that God is love on a cross, and that God is to be loved in all our "crosses." Of His cross He made a Mass that satisfied God, saved and sanctified men. Of our "crosses" we are to do the same. That is the only way we can be merry in time or in eternity; the only way we can ever enjoy Christmas on earth or in heaven; the only way we can receive God's greeting at Christmas time and adequately return it.

Date Due

JUL 23 '56	NOV 1 9 '58	DE 1 1 '61	NOV 2 4 1980
JUL 2 5 '56	EC 1 5 '58	DE 18 '61	
OCT 3 '56	AN 2 1 '59	JA 3 '62	
DEC 1 0 '56	JAN 2 6 '59	JA 1 8 '62	
DEC 1 7 '56	APR 6 '59	MR 1 '62	
JAN 9 '57	APR 2 4 '59	MR 18 '62	
JAN 3 0 '57	JUN 2 5 '59	JY 5 '62	
FEB 1 5 '57	JUL 1 0 '59	JY 20 '62	
MAR 2 0 '57	JUL 2 5 '59	FEB 8 '63	
MAY 2 2 '57	AUG 1 4 '59	SE 26 '63	
JUN 7 '57	DEC 1 6 '59	DE 16 '63	
JUL 5 '57	JE 2 0 '60	DE 1 4 '64	
JUL 1 8	JY 20 '60	MY 1 7 '65	
SEP 2 5 '57	AG 1 '60	AG 4 '65	
DEC 1 1 '57	JA 1 9 '61	JA 5 '67	
JUN 2 3 '58	JUN 2 2 P.M.	FE 1 8 '67	
JUL 7 '58	JY 8 '61	DE 8 '85	
JUL 1 4 '58	AG 1 4 '61		